The Fundamentals of
DRAWING
PORTRAITS

The Fundamentals of
DRAWING
PORTRAITS

A PRACTICAL AND INSPIRATIONAL COURSE

Barrington Barber

Capella

This edition published in 2006 by Arcturus Publishing Limited
26/27 Bickels Yard, 151–153 Bermondsey Street,
London SE1 3HA

ISBN-13: 978-1-84193-319-1
ISBN-10: 1-84193-319-8

Printed in China

Contents

Introduction

WHAT IS A PORTRAIT? It is said that Picasso produced a Cubist portrait of a friend and when this was shown to Matisse he could not identify the person. Picasso then stuck a moustache onto the picture and Matisse could immediately see the likeness. This story exemplifies a fundamental of portraiture: no matter how far from an exact likeness a drawing may be, it must contain some recognizable form of the person. In order to capture this you will need to spend a lot of time in direct observation, noting the particular image of a human being that your subject represents.

How much you should flatter or be brutally honest with your subject when drawing is a perennial question. If they, like Cromwell, want a portrait 'warts and all' then the more objective you can be the better. However, very few people are honest enough about their own appearance to be able to live with the consequences of this approach, and so most portrait artists try to give the best possible view of the sitter. This may mean altering the light effects, changing the position of the head slightly, getting the sitter to relax, and employing other small ways of helping to ease tension out of the face and bring some agreeable element into prominence. Fortunately, most people have some good feature that can be the focal point of a portrait, allowing the artist to slightly reduce the prominence of a tense mouth, a weak chin or rather protruding ears or nose. The ravages of time have also to be taken into account, although lines, creases or sagging flesh can be slightly softened to give a more acceptable version which is still recognizable.

Throughout this book I have tried to choose portraits which are sometimes famous but always interesting. You will find a range of approaches, and within the examples from each valuable lessons to absorb and take from. There isn't a portrait in this collection that can't teach us something about the way to approach depicting the features of your friends, family, acquaintances and even complete strangers. What I hope you will also come to realize is that although the measurable differences between all the faces portrayed are really very minute, the appearances are immensely varied. The human face has an extraordinary ability to mirror all the expressions and emotions capable of recognition. It is this facility which artists have striven for generations to explore in myriad ways.

What comes out of this exploration does, of course, depend on the skill of the artist. The only way to reach the level of skill required to produce good portraits is to practise drawing. The more you practise, the better you will get. If you can't regularly practise drawing faces, any type of drawing is a valid way to increase your skills. Even an object of still life, such as a pot, can be approached as if you were drawing a portrait. This would mean looking for the specific characteristics of the pot in the situation you have devised. The characteristics will only be evident when the pot is in that particular position, with that particular lighting and related to those particular surroundings. Change the situation, the lighting and the surroundings and you will have a different portrait. This is why so many artists find portraiture endlessly fascinating. There really is no limit to the possibilities for expression it offers.

Barrington Barber

Wimbledon, February 2003

First Steps

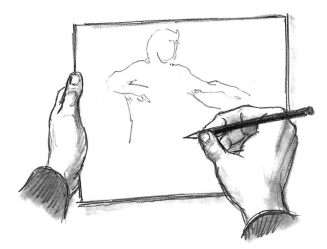

IN THIS FIRST SECTION we look at the most important aspects of drawing portraits. Themes are presented in the order in which you will tackle them, so that even if you have never done a portrait before you will know how to proceed. You will notice that much emphasis is placed on the structure of the head and the features. When you sit in front of a subject, you will carefully observe the particular image of a human being that this person represents. In order to be able to gauge the person accurately, you must have knowledge of what you are looking at. For example, the main shape of the head is vital because if you ignore this the resulting drawing will never really catch the qualities of the sitter. Basic anatomical and structural drawings have been provided to help you analyze this major basic shape. If you are very new to portrait drawing, you will find it beneficial to practise drawing just that shape accurately if loosely and lightly.

The particular arrangement of features is also very important. If you are keen to do so, you can measure everything, and this can help greatly in producing a good likeness. However, measurement by itself will only give the proportion, and you should aim to use your drawing practice as your guide to how the features relate and fit together.

The next important aspect to work on is the shape of each feature. Obviously each of us sees things slightly differently from the next person. Nevertheless there is an objective shape that a particular face will have which can be studied until correctly drawn. How each lump or bump in each feature is related to the whole shape and whether the curves are greater or smaller can make a lot of difference to the final result. There is no substitute for careful observation. If you practise looking at people's faces it will enormously enhance your ability to recognize and draw the shapes in front of you. Changing light conditions and changing expressions give subtle variations to the features. You have to decide exactly which of these variations to include in your drawing.

Finally, we look at a range of materials, to give you a wide spectrum of options. What you discover for yourself through trial and error will stay with you and inform your work in the future.

The Angle of the Head

The most distinctive part of any portrait is the face, which is where the likeness and characteristics of the sitter can be shown most easily. This is your starting point. The head should be dealt with as a whole so that the face has a solid basis. Only so many views of the head are possible for a portrait to be recognizable.

The position you choose for the head will make a lot of difference to the end result, and whether people recognize your subject. We will start with the most common, and then assess the workable alternatives.

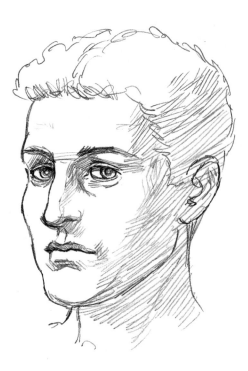

The three-quarter view is probably the most popular position. It gives a clear view of the eyes and enough of the shape of the nose to give a good likeness.

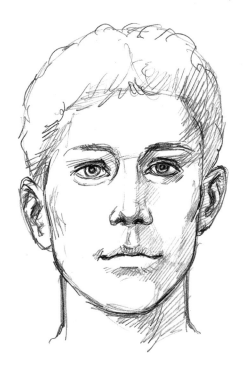

Full face, from the same eye level as the artist, is excellent for capturing the expression in the eyes, but the shape of the nose is less obvious.

The head seen in profile allows clear defini-tion of the features. Generally, though, por-traits from this angle are less expressive, because the eyes are not clearly seen.

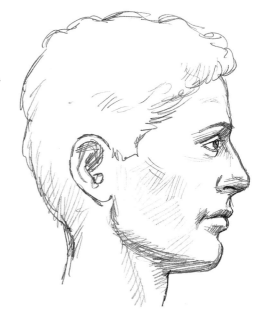

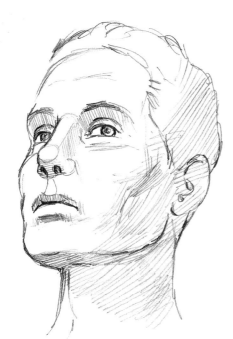

The head tilted back a little gives an air of coolness, even haughtiness, but it's worth considering.

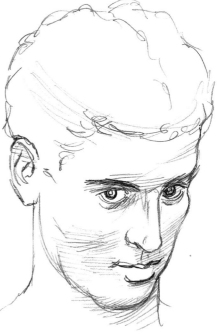

The head tilted forward can give a rather quizzical or defensive expression.

Drawing the Head: Basic Method

The basic shapes and areas of the head have to be taken into account when you start to draw your portrait. There are five basic steps. These will give you a strong shape which you can then work over to get the subtle individual shapes and marks that will make your drawing a realistic representation of the person you are drawing.

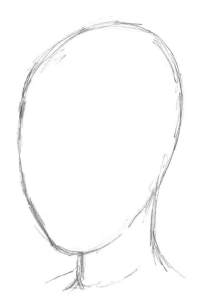

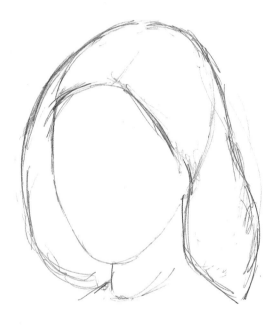

First ascertain the overall shape of the head or skull and the way it sits on the neck. It may be very rounded, long and thin or square and solid. Whatever its shape you need to define it clearly and accurately at the outset, as this will make everything else easier later on.

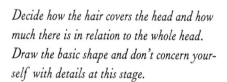

Decide how the hair covers the head and how much there is in relation to the whole head. Draw the basic shape and don't concern your-self with details at this stage.

Now ascertain the basic shape and position of the features, starting with the eyes. Get the level and size correct and their general shape, including the eyebrows.

The nose is next, its shape (whether upturned, straight, aquiline, broad or narrow), its tilt and the amount it projects from the main surface of the face.

Now look at the mouth, gauging its width and thick-ness, and ensuring that you place it correctly in relation to the chin.

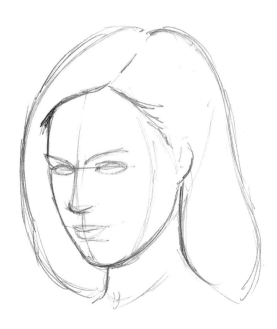

The form of the face is shown by the tonal qualities of the shadows on the head. Just outline the form and concentrate on capturing the general area correctly.

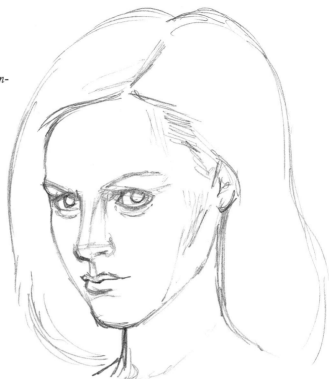

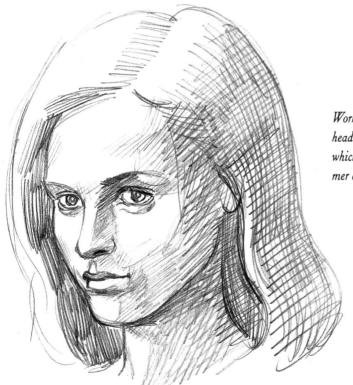

Work in the tonal values over the whole head, noting which areas are darker and which are not so dark, emphasizing the former and softening the latter.

Drawing the Head: Alternative Method

An alternative method for beginning a portrait is to work from the centre of the features and move outwards toward the edges. This approach is appropriate for both fairly confident draughtsmen and beginners, and is very helpful if you are not too sure about judging proportions and measuring distances.

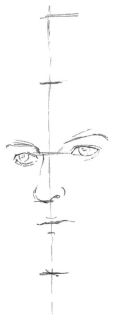

Phase Two: Defining the Features

● *Draw in the shapes of the eyes and eyebrows, ensuring they are correctly placed. Notice how the eye nearest to you is seen more full on than the eye further away. You can try to define the point where the further eyebrow meets the edge of the head as seen from your position.*

● *The nose now needs to be carefully drawn in: its outside shape, and also – in lightly drawn lines – how the form creates shadows on the unlit side.*

● *Positionally the ear fits between the levels of the eye and the nose, but is off to the side. Gauge how the distance between the eye and the ear relates to the length of the nose and put in the outline shape of the ear.*

● *Shape the mouth. The half of the mouth on the further side of the face will not look as long as the half of the mouth on the facing side. The centre of the mouth must be in line with the centre of the nostrils. Draw in the pointed part of the chin.*

For this exercise we will assume that we are drawing a three-quarter view. Start by drawing a vertical line on a sheet of paper and then make a mark at the top and bottom of it. Now follow the steps shown in the following series of illustrations. Look carefully at your model throughout the exercise.

Phase One: Marking out the Features

● *Mark a horizontal line for the position of the eyes, halfway between the top and bottom marks. Roughly draw in the relative position and shapes of the eyes.*

● *Make a mark halfway between the top mark and the level of the eye for the position of the hairline.*

● *A mark halfway between the level of the eye and the bottom mark will give you the position of the end of the nose. Draw in a very simple shape to give you a clear idea of its shape. The top mark denoting the top of the head will appear rather to one side of your vertical line.*

● *The bottom line marks the point of the chin, which will be on the vertical line.*

● *The position of the mouth has to be calculated next. The mouth is nearer to the nose than it is to the chin, so don't put it halfway between them; if you are not sure, measure with the rule of thumb method (see page 33).*

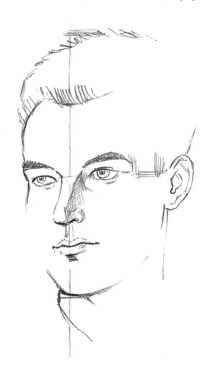

Phase Three: Outlining Shadows

● *Trace out the shape of the shadows running down the side of the head facing you. Don't make the lines too heavy; just outline the edge of the shadow faintly from the forehead down round the cheekbone, the outside of the mouth and onto the chin. Indicate the neck and its shadow outline.*
● *Put in the shadow around the eyes, nose and, where they are needed, the mouth. Softly shade in the whole area including the hair area and the neck. Define the edges of the back of the head and neck and on the opposite side where the brow stands out against the background. Complete the shape of the top of the head.*
● *Put in the whole of the shape down the edge of the face furthest away from you; be careful not to make the chin jut out too far. Check the accuracy by looking at the distance between the line of the nose and the outline of the cheekbone and then the corner of the mouth on the further side and the edge of the face and chin related to it. Make any corrections. At this stage your drawing should look like a simple version of your sitter.*

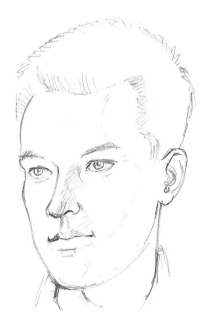

Phase Four: Applying Tonal Values

● *Begin by darkening the areas that stand out most clearly. Carefully model the tone around the form so that where there is a strong contrast you increase the darkness of the tone and where there is less contrast you soften it, even rubbing it out*

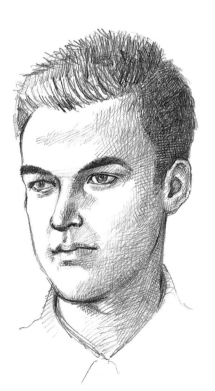

if necessary. Build up the tonal values with care, ensuring that in the areas where there is a gradual shift from dark to light you reflect this in the way you apply tone.
● *The most definition in the features should be the shape of the eyes, sometimes the eyebrows, and the corner between the nose and eye and around the nostrils. The most definite part of the mouth is where it opens, and sometimes the area just below the lower lip. The edge of the chin is often quite well defined, depending on the sort of light you have.*
● *Mark in the clearer strands in the hair; and the outer and inner shapes of the ear. Look at the setting of the head on the shoulders, noting how the shoulders slope away from the neck on both sides of the head.*
● *You may find that the background behind the lighter side of the head looks dark and the background behind the darker side of the head looks lighter. A darker background can help to project the face forward. Finish off by applying delicate touches – either with the pencil or a good rubber – to soften the edges of the tones.*

The Male Head: Working Out Proportions

For beginners especially it can be very helpful to use a grid as a guide on which to map out the head, to ensure that the proportions are correct. Despite the amazing variety of faces found in the world, the proportions shown here are broadly true of all adult humans from any race or culture, unless there is major deformation, and so can be used for anyone you care to use as a model. Obviously there will be slight differences but so minute as to be safely disregarded. The only proviso is that the head must be straight and upright, either full face or fully in profile. If the head is at an angle the proportions will distort.

The number of units varies depending on whether you are drawing the head full on or in profile. Study each example with its accompanying notes before trying to use the system as a basis for your portraits.

Horizontal Reading: Full Face

For the full-face examples a proportion of five units across and seven units down has been used. Before you begin to study the individual units, note the central line drawn vertically down the length of the face. This passes at equi-distance between the eyes, and centrally through the nose, mouth and chin.

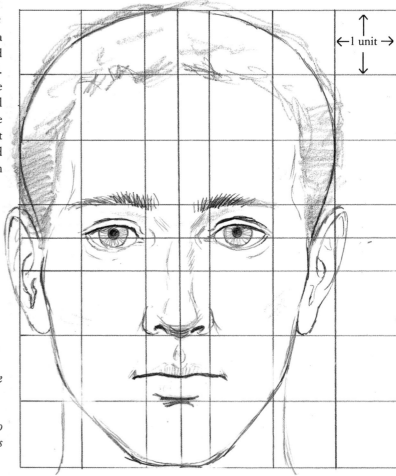

← 1 unit →

- *The width of the eye is one-fifth of the width of the whole head and is equal to 1 unit.*

- *The space between the eyes is 1 unit.*

- *The edge of the head to the outside corner of the eye is 1 unit.*

- *The outside corner of the eye to the inside corner of the eye is 1 unit.*

- *The inside corner of the left eye to the inside corner of the right eye is 1 unit.*

- *The inside corner of the right eye to its outside corner is 1 unit.*

- *The outside corner of the right eye to the edge of the head is 1 unit.*

- *The central unit contains the nose and is also the width of the square base of the chin or jaw.*

Vertical Reading: Full Face

- *Eyes: halfway down the length of the head.*
- *Hairline: 1 unit from the top of the head.*
- *Nose: one and a half units from the level of the eyes downwards.*
- *Bottom of the lower lip: 1 unit up from the edge of the jawbone.*
- *Ears: the length of the nose, plus the distance from the eye-line to the eyebrows is 2 units.*

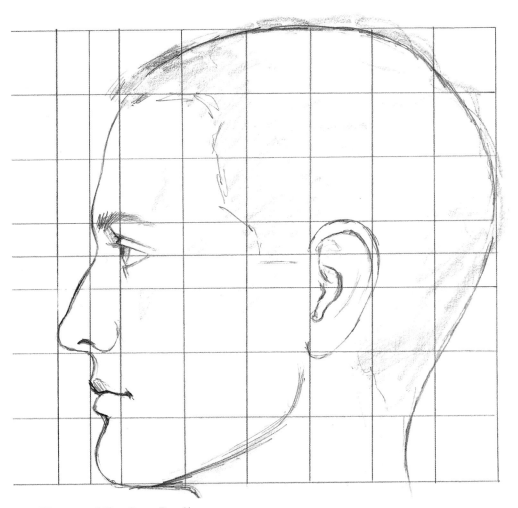

Horizontal Reading: Profile

- *The head in profile is 7 units wide and 7 units long, including the nose.*

- *The front edge of the eye is 1 unit back from the point of the nose.*

- *The ear is 1 unit in width. Its front edge is 4 units from the point of the nose and 2 units from the back edge of the head.*

- *The nose projects half of 1 unit from the front of the main skull shape, which is about six and a half units wide in profile.*

The Female Head: Working out Proportions

These examples have been drawn to exactly the same size as those on the preceding spread. Generally the female head is smaller than the male but the proportions are exactly the same. (Also see page 34 for information on the head proportions of children, which at certain ages are significantly different from those of adults.)

Horizontal Reading: Full Face

For the full-face examples a proportion of five units across and seven units down has been used. Before you begin to study the individual units, note the central line drawn vertically down the length of the face. This passes at equi-distance between the eyes, and centrally through the nose, mouth and chin.

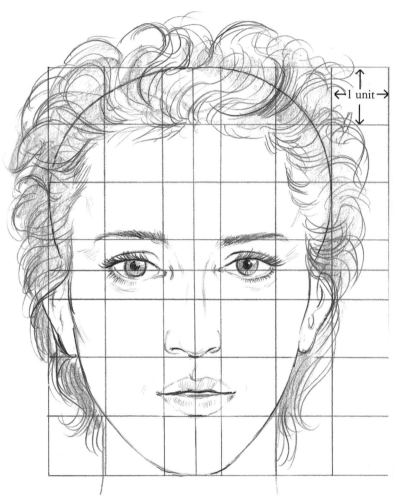

- *The width of the eye is one-fifth of the width of the whole head and is equal to 1 unit.*

- *The space between the eyes is 1 unit.*

- *The edge of the head to the outside corner of the eye is 1 unit.*

- *The outside corner of the eye to the inside corner of the eye is 1 unit.*

- *The inside corner of the left eye to the inside corner of the right eye is 1 unit.*

- *The inside corner of the right eye to its outside corner is 1 unit.*

- *The outside corner of the right eye to the edge of the head is 1 unit.*

- *The central unit contains the nose and is also the width of the square base of the chin or jaw.*

Vertical Reading: Full Face

- *Eyes: halfway down the length of the head.*
- *Hairline: 1 unit from the top of the head.*
- *Nose: one and a half units from the level of the eyes downwards.*
- *Bottom of the lower lip: 1 unit up from the edge of the jawbone.*
- *Ears: the length of the nose, plus the distance from the eye-line to the eyebrows is 2 units.*

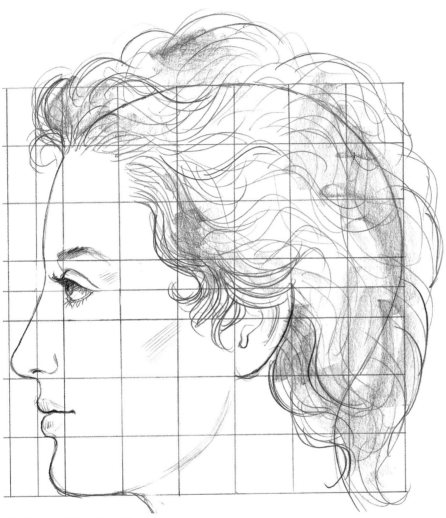

Horizontal Reading: Profile

- *The head in profile is 7 units wide and 7 units long, including the nose.*

- *The front edge of the eye is 1 unit back from the point of the nose.*

- *The ear is 1 unit in width. Its front edge is 4 units from the point of the nose and 2 units from the back edge of the head.*

- *The nose projects half of 1 unit from the front of the main skull shape, which is about six and a half units wide in profile.*

Practice: Drawing the Head and Features

In this exercise we are going to practise drawing different views of the heads. You can either use the model shown or choose another to draw. Make sure the features line up horizontally across the three views, otherwise there will be discrepancies in their relationship. Before you begin you will find it helpful to define the form of the face by marking in the edges of the planes on the face, particularly the outlines of the eye sockets and eyelids, the mouth and the formation of the bridge, length and tip of the nose.

This exercise can also be used to practise getting the shapes of the features right. Detailed drawings of the principal features – eyes, nose and mouth – are provided opposite. Periodically check your effort against the drawings and the accompanying annotations.

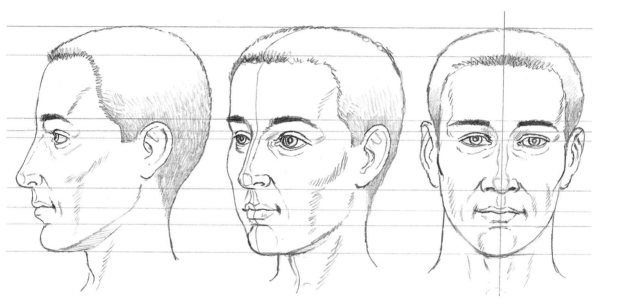

Profile view

- *The nose projects much further than the rest of the face.*
- *The jaw projects no further than the forehead.*
- *The ear is positioned well back past the halfway mark of the profile.*
- *From this viewpoint the line of the mouth is quite short.*
- *Study the shape of the eye.*

Three-quarter view

- *The further eye has a slightly different conformation to the nearer eye, mainly because you can see the inside corner of the near eye, so the length of the eye is more obvious.*
- *The mouth shape is shorter on the far side of the central line and longer on the near side of the central line.*
- *The same observation applies to the eyebrows.*

Full face view

- *The eyes are one eye-length apart*
- *The two sides of the head tend to mirror each other.*
- *The widest part of the head is above the ears.*
- *The widest part of the face is at cheekbone level.*
- *The ears are less obvious from this perspective.*

The Features Close Up

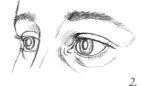
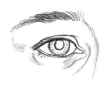
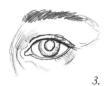

1.

2.

3.

Eyes

Seen in profile the eye is a relatively simple shape to draw, and yet many people get it wrong, tending to draw something they recognize as an eye instead of the actual shape.

1. Profile view
The eyelids should project beyond the curve of the eyeball: if they didn't project, the eye could not close.

2. Three-quarter view
Note a marked difference in the shapes. The further eye is closer to the profile view in that the eyelid projects past the eyeball on the outside corner. On the nearer eye, because the inside corner is visible, the shape appears to be more complete. The far eyebrow appears shorter than the near one.

3. Frontal view
From this angle the eyes are more or less a mirror image. The space between them is the same as the horizontal length of the eye. Note that normally about one-eighth to one-quarter of the iris is hidden under the upper eyelid, and the bottom edge just touches the lower lid.

Nose

The nose at different angles presents marked differences in shape. In very young people the nostrils are the only areas that stand out.

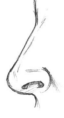
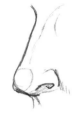

1.

2.

3.

1. Profile view
The main observation here concerns the shape of the nostril and its relationship to the point of the nose.

2. Three-quarter view
The outline shape is still evident but notice how its relationship to the nostril has changed.

3. Frontal view
The only shapes visible are the surface of the length of the nose and the point. The nostrils are the most clearly defined areas, so note their relationship.

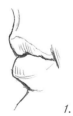
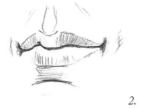
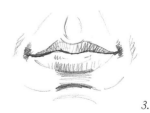

1.

2.

3.

Mouth

1. Profile view
The line of the mouth (where the lips part) is at its shortest in this view. Note whether the upper lip projects further than the lower lip, or vice versa, or whether they project similarly.

2. Three-quarter view
The angle accounts for the difference in the curves of top and bottom lip. The nearer side appears almost as it does straight on, whereas the farther side is shortened due to the angle.

3. Frontal view
This view is the one we are most familiar with. The line of the mouth is very important to draw accurately – you need to capture its shape precisely or the lips will not look right.

Measuring the Head

The surest way of increasing your understanding of the head, and becoming adept at portraying its features accurately, is to practise drawing it life size, from life. It is very difficult to draw the head in miniature without first having gained adequate experience of drawing it at exactly the size it is in reality, but this is what beginning artists tend to do, in the mistaken belief that somehow it will be easier.

Getting to know the head involves mapping it out, and this means taking measurements from clearly defined points to clearly defined points. For the next exercise you will need a live model, a measuring device, such as a ruler or callipers, a pencil and a large sheet of paper.

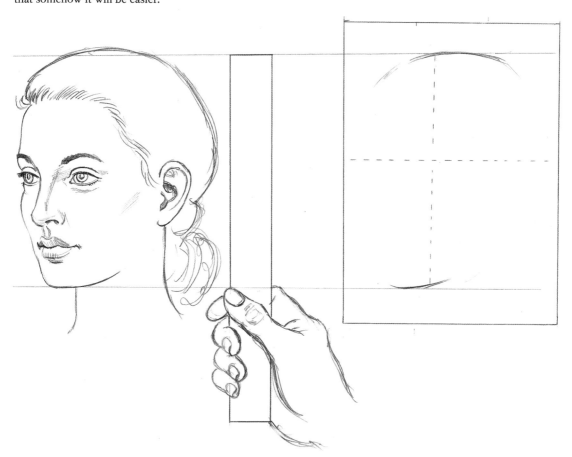

Measure the length of the head from the highest point to the tip of the chin. Mark your measurement on the paper. Measure the width of the head at the widest point; this is usually across the area just above the ears, certainly if viewed full on from the front. Mark this measurement on the paper. The whole head should fit inside the vertical and horizontal measurements you have transferred to your drawing paper.

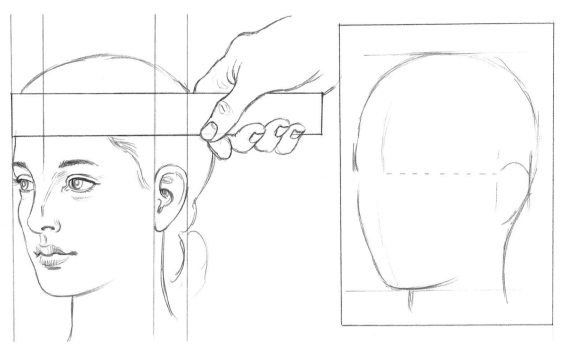

Measure the eye level. This should be about halfway down the full length of the vertical, unless the head is tilted. Decide the angle you are going to look at the head.

Assuming it is a three-quarter view, the next measurement is critical: it is the distance from the centre between the eyes to the front edge of the ear.

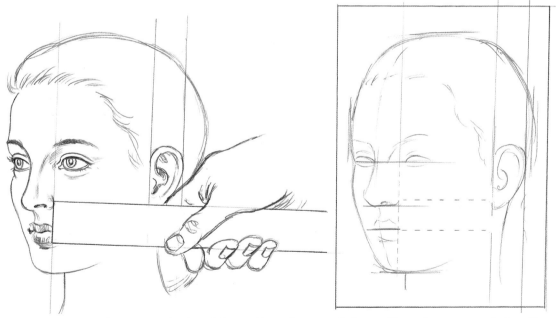

Measure the distance from the outside edge of the nostril to the front edge of the ear. Mark it and then place the shape of the ear and the position of both eyes. Check the actual length of the nose from the inside corner of the eye down to the base of the nostril. Next measure the line of

the centre of the mouth's opening; you can calculate this either from the base of the nose or from the point of the chin. Mark it in. Now measure from the corner of the mouth facing you to a line projecting down the jawbone under the ear. Mark it.

Assessing the Features

The measurements you have taken in the previous exercises will provide very accurate proportions for you to work to when drawing the features. When you have sketched out roughly where every feature begins and ends, look carefully at the shapes of each of them and then draw them in.

The eyes are paramount, because often they are what makes a person recognizable to us. The mouth and nose are next. The pecking order of the rest depends on the characteristics of your subject. The illustrations below show the main points and relationships to consider when drawing the features.

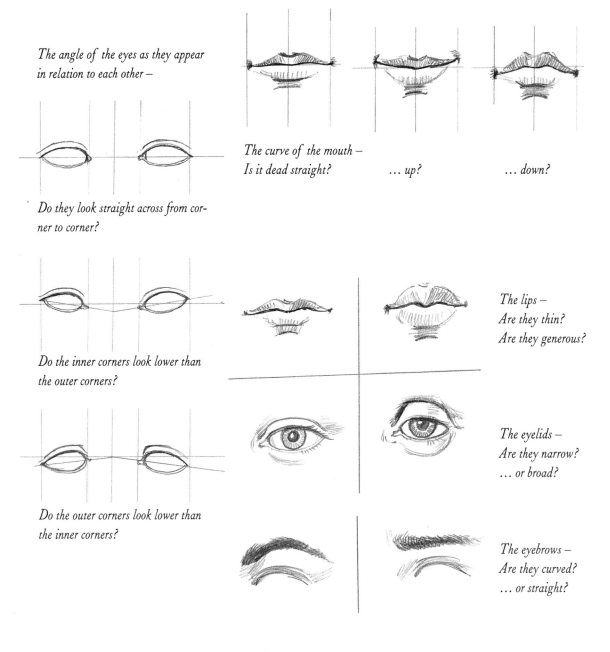

The angle of the eyes as they appear in relation to each other –

Do they look straight across from corner to corner?

The curve of the mouth –
Is it dead straight?   *… up?*   *… down?*

Do the inner corners look lower than the outer corners?

The lips –
Are they thin?
Are they generous?

Do the outer corners look lower than the inner corners?

The eyelids –
Are they narrow?
… or broad?

The eyebrows –
Are they curved?
… or straight?

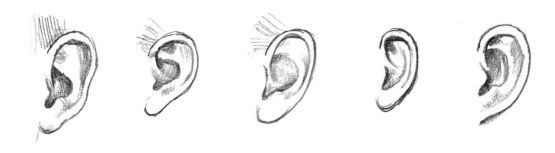

The ears –
These come in a variety of permutations; here are a few for you to consider.

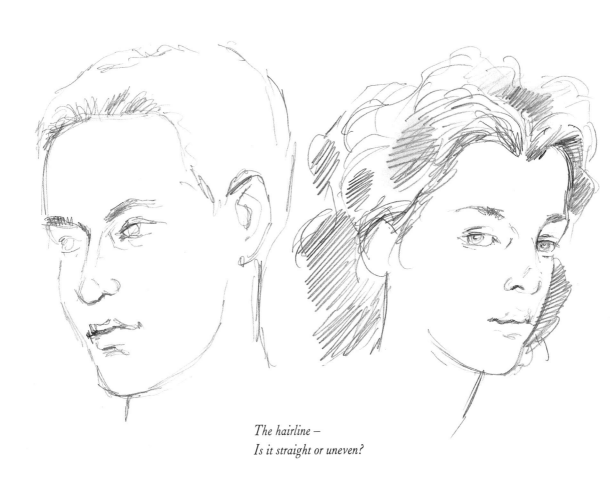

The hairline –
Is it straight or uneven?

Connecting with the Viewer

The aim of all portrait artists is to engage the interest of an audience beyond the relative few who actually know the subject of their drawing or painting. The really great ones manage to lift any subject out of the ordinary rut of existence and invest him or her with a humanity that we viewers connect with. The features, especially the eyes and mouth, are what draw us in. In both examples shown here a fleeting expression has been captured which we cannot read with any certainty. It is worth trying to practise drawing difficult expressions, such as these, and the subtlety of tone they require.

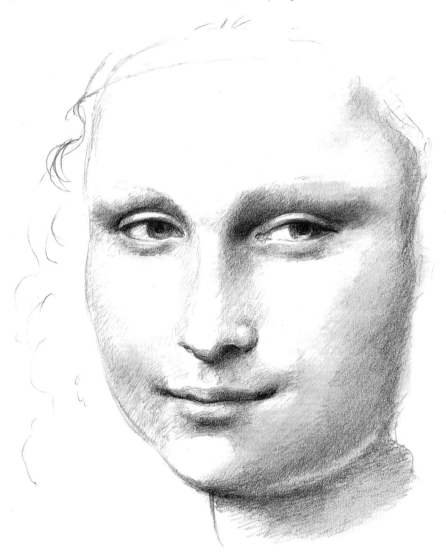

Leonardo's La Giaconda, or Mona Lisa, is probably the most famous painting in the world. The wife of an important Florentine, the sitter has become a symbol of the mystery of womanhood and the epitome of subtle charm. The whole portrait is of great power, but it is her mysterious smile that is the focus of most interest, and of this pared-down copy. The effect is created by Leonardo's famed sfumato technique in which soft, shadowy tones gently melt one form into another without any jarring notes. Every other artist since da Vinci has employed sfumato. Very few though have been able to equal his handling of it.

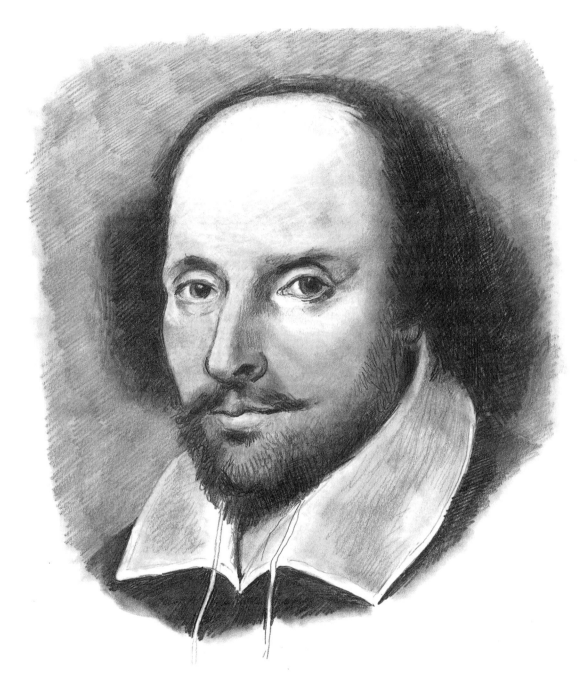

The original of this drawing of William Shakespeare, by John Taylor, is believed to have been taken from life, and is perhaps the only record we have of the playwright's likeness. Taylor was little known, but he must have learnt his trade well to be able to produce a portrait of such depth. The intensity of the gaze and the shadows around the face are very well drawn devices. Shakespeare was a man of mystery, and Taylor's handling of the tone helps to create this effect. The direct gaze seems to hold both humour and wisdom, and the ear-ring beneath the curtain of black hair lends the subject an air of bohemianism.

Bones of the Head

We need to remind ourselves frequently when drawing portraits that what we see is due entirely to structures that are for the most part hidden from view. This is particularly true of the bones that underlie the skin and muscles. An understanding of the landscape of the skull is necessary if we are to draw good portraits. Look at the features identified on the drawings below and see if you can find them on your own head by feel.

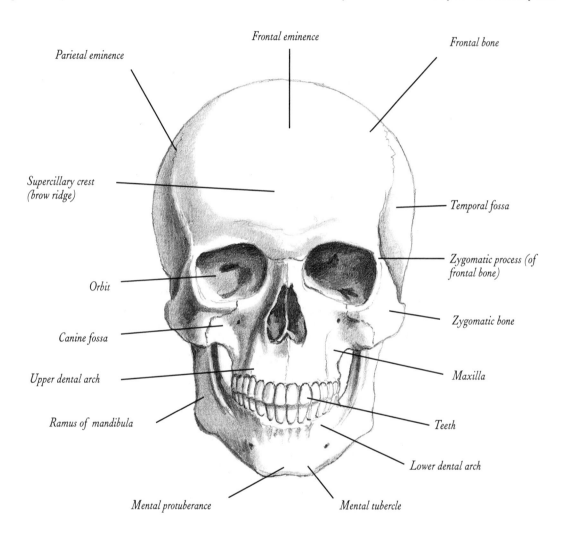

Frontal eminence

Frontal bone

Parietal eminence

Supercillary crest (brow ridge)

Temporal fossa

Zygomatic process (of frontal bone)

Orbit

Zygomatic bone

Canine fossa

Upper dental arch

Maxilla

Ramus of mandibula

Teeth

Lower dental arch

Mental protuberance

Mental tubercle

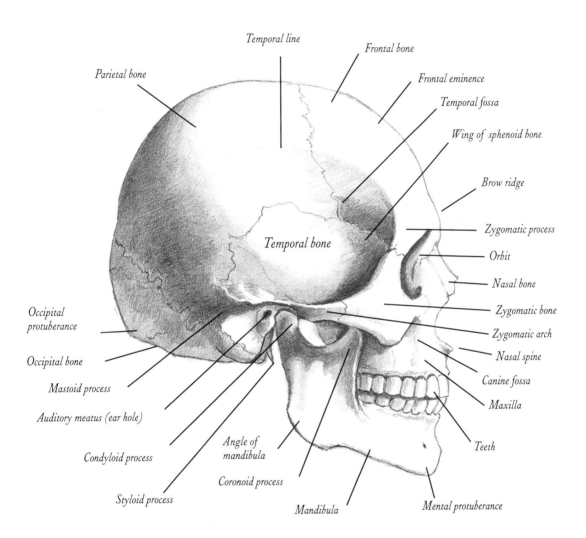

Temporal line

Frontal bone

Parietal bone

Frontal eminence

Temporal fossa

Wing of sphenoid bone

Brow ridge

Zygomatic process

Temporal bone

Orbit

Nasal bone

Occipital protuberance

Zygomatic bone

Zygomatic arch

Nasal spine

Occipital bone

Canine fossa

Mastoid process

Maxilla

Auditory meatus (ear hole)

Teeth

Condyloid process

Angle of mandibula

Coronoid process

Styloid process

Mandibula

Mental protuberance

Skull and Facial Muscles

Movement and expression are two principal elements of portraiture and both are governed by the muscles. It is important to know where the bones and muscles are and how they behave if we are to produce portraits of character and individuality. Study the following illustrations and the accompanying annotations. Don't worry about learning the names, although you may find that giving each muscle an identity helps you to remember where it is and the function it performs.

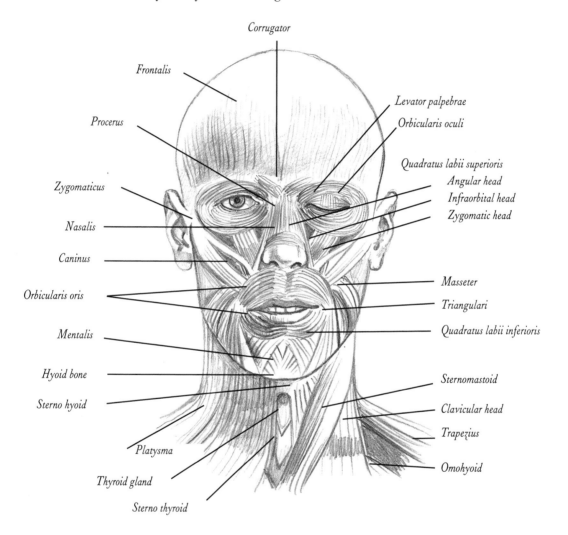

Corrugator

Frontalis

Procerus

Zygomaticus

Nasalis

Caninus

Orbicularis oris

Mentalis

Hyoid bone

Sterno hyoid

Platysma

Thyroid gland

Sterno thyroid

Levator palpebrae

Orbicularis oculi

Quadratus labii superioris

Angular head

Infraorbital head

Zygomatic head

Masseter

Triangulari

Quadratus labii inferioris

Sternomastoid

Clavicular head

Trapezius

Omohyoid

Muscle/Function

Corrugator: Pulls eyebrows together
Orbicularis oculi: Closes eyes
Quadratus labii superioris: Raises upper lip
Orbicularis oris: Closes mouth and purses lips
Mentalis: Moves skin of chin
Masseter: Upward traction of lower jaw; energetic closing of mouth

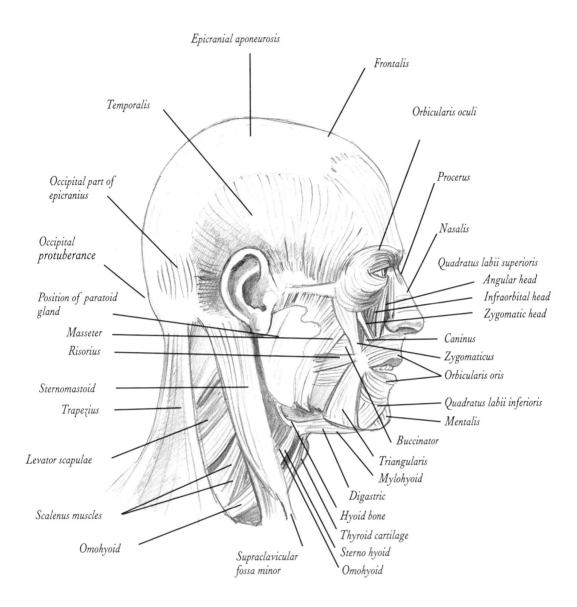

Epicranial aponeurosis

Frontalis

Orbicularis oculi

Temporalis

Procerus

Nasalis

Occipital part of epicranius

Quadratus labii superioris

Angular head

Infraorbital head

Zygomatic head

Occipital protuberance

Position of paratoid gland

Caninus

Zygomaticus

Orbicularis oris

Masseter

Risorius

Quadratus labii inferioris

Mentalis

Sternomastoid

Trapezius

Buccinator

Triangularis

Mylohyoid

Levator scapulae

Digastric

Scalenus muscles

Hyoid bone

Thyroid cartilage

Sterno hyoid

Omohyoid

Omohyoid

Supraclavicular fossa minor

Muscle/Function

Occipital part of epicranius: Backward traction of epicranial aponeurosis and skin

Frontal part of epicranius: Moves skin on top of head

Compressor nasi: Narrows nostrils; downward traction of nose

Levator angulis oris: Raises angle of mouth

Zygomaticus major: Energetic upward traction of angle of mouth

Depressor anguli oris: Downward traction of angle of mouth

Depressor labii inferioris: Energetic downward pull of lower lip

Trapezius risorius: Lateral pulling of angle of mouth

Temporalis: Similar action to that of masseter – see opposite

Buccinator: Lateral traction of angle of mouth; evacuation of fluid or air from between teeth and cheeks

The Figure: Proportions

If you are considering tackling a full-figure portrait you will need to be as aware of the proportions of the body as you are of the proportions of the head. Proportions vary, depending on the position of the body. The system of measurement of the body is the classical proportion, but this is applicable only if the figure is standing straight with the head held erect. For any other pose you must rely on eye and the rule of thumb method of measurement (see opposite).

Classical proportion is worked out on the basis of the length of one head fitting into the height of the body eight times, as shown below. The bottom of the pelvis marks the midway point. The knees are about two head lengths from the centre point. When the arm is hanging down loosely, the fingertips should be about one head length from the midway point.

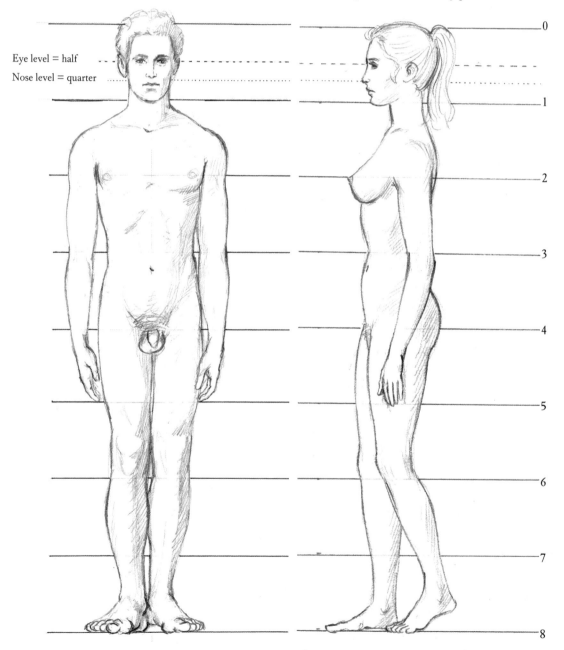

Eye level = half

Nose level = quarter

0

1

2

3

4

5

6

7

8

Rule of Thumb Method of Measurement

When drawing at sight size – the size a figure or object looks from where you are standing – the proportions can be gauged by using the rule of thumb method. Take the measurement by holding your arm outstretched with your pencil upright in line with the drawing board (see illustration below). Once the measurement has been taken, you can then transfer it to your drawing paper. You must ensure that you measure everything in your drawing in the same way, keeping the same distance from your model and your pencil extended at arm's length. If you do this, the method will give you a fairly accurate range of proportions. Deviate from this, however, and you will find your proportions looking decidedly out of kilter.

The rule of thumb method can also be used when drawing larger than sight size, by extrapolating from the proportions. However, only experienced artists should attempt this. And my advice to beginners would be that in all circumstances the method is of limited value to you. For those in the early stages of learning to draw it is always helpful and instructive to draw much larger than rule of thumb allows, at larger than life size preferably, so that mistakes can be seen clearly and the necessary corrections made. Big is most certainly better for beginners. Drawing large should never be regarded as not 'proper' art. It can be a very liberating and instructive experience for artists of all abilities.

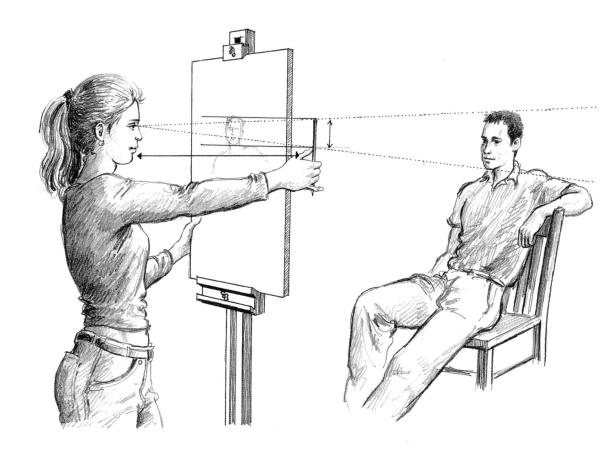

The Proportions of Children

There are significant proportional differences between the bodies of children and those of adults which the artist has to bear in mind when undertaking a portrait. One of the most obvious differences is seen in the head, which in an adult is about twice as large as that of a two-year-old. The features, too, change with growth.

In adults the eyes are closer together and are set halfway down the head. Nose, cheekbones and jaw become more clearly defined and more angular as we mature.

Study the following drawings and note how the body – and especially the head – changes with growth.

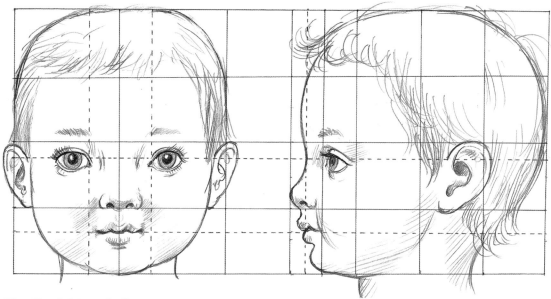

The Head: Major Differences

- In relation to its body, a child's head is much larger; this will be evident even if you can only see the head and shoulders. A child's head is much smaller than an adult's, but the proportion of head to body is such that the head appears larger.

- The cranium or upper part of the child's skull is much larger in proportion to the rest of the face. This gradually alters as the child grows and reaches adult proportions.

- The child's eyes appear much larger in the head than an adult's, whereas the mouth and nose often appear smaller. The eyes also appear to be wider apart. The nose is usually short with nostrils facing outward so that it appears upturned. This is because the nasal bones are not developed.

- The jawbones and teeth are much smaller in proportion to the rest of the head, again because they are still not fully developed. The rule with the adult – that places the eyes halfway down the head – does not work with a child, where the eyes appear much lower down.

- With very young children, the forehead is high and wide, the ears and eyes very large, the nose small and upturned, the cheeks full and round and the mouth and jaw very small. Also there are no lines to speak of on the face.

- The hair is finer, even if luxuriant, and so tends to show the head shape much more clearly.

The Figure: Proportions

The classical unit of measurement, the head, has been used to gauge the figure proportions of children at various ages. The adult length is about 8 lengths of the head.

At Two Years
- *Proportion: 3¹/₄ lengths of the head into the length of the body*
- *The baby's head is smaller than the other two heads and about half the size of an adult head*

At Six Years
- *Proportion: 5 lengths of the head into the length of the body*

At Twelve Years
- *Proportion: 5¹/₂ lengths of the head into the length of the body*
- *The head is still growing. The adult head is slightly bigger than the head at this age*

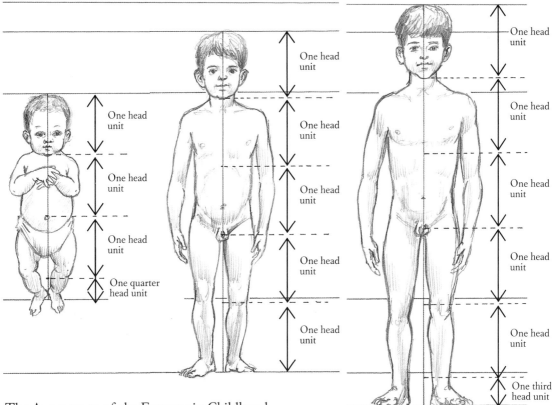

The Appearance of the Features in Childhood

At Two Years
- *High clear forehead, hairline well back at top and sides, hair fine*
- *Eyes separated by more than length of eye, and lower than halfway*
- *Ears proportionally lower*
- *Nostrils obvious*
- *Jawline and cheeks very round*

At Six Years
- *More hair, encroaching on forehead; head larger*
- *Jawbone more developed*
- *Eyebrows thicker*
- *Eyes higher up*
- *Nose, mouth and ears higher*
- *Jawbone still rounded*

At Twelve Years
- *Hair thicker*
- *Head larger still*
- *Ears full size, still low on head*
- *Jawbone looking squarer or sharper*

Your First Portrait Step-by-Step

When you are confident of your ability to draw the features accurately, you are ready to try your hand at a full-scale portrait. If you are very lucky someone may commission you to draw a portrait, but it is more likely you will have to initiate the event yourself, especially in the beginning.

You will need to agree on a number of sittings with your sitter, and how long each of these should last; two or three sittings of between 30 minutes and one hour should be sufficient. It is advisable not to let your subject get too bored with sitting, because dullness may creep into their expression and therefore into your portrait.

Once the schedule has been decided, it is time to start work. First, make several drawings of your subject's face and head, plus the rest of the body if that is required, from several different angles. Aim to capture the shape and form clearly and unambiguously. In addition to making these drawings, take photographs: front and three-quarter views are necessary and possibly also a profile view.

All this information is to help you decide which is the best view of the sitter, and how much of their figure you want to show. The preliminary sketching will also help you to get the feel of how their features appear, and shape your ideas of what you want to bring out in the finished work. Changing light conditions and changing expressions will give subtle variations to each feature. You have to decide exactly which of these variations to include in the drawing.

Draw the face from left and right and also in profile.

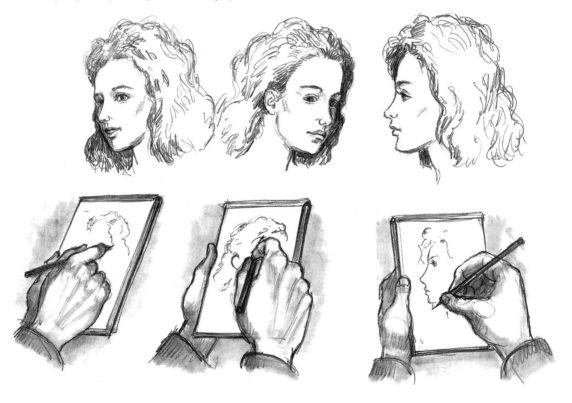

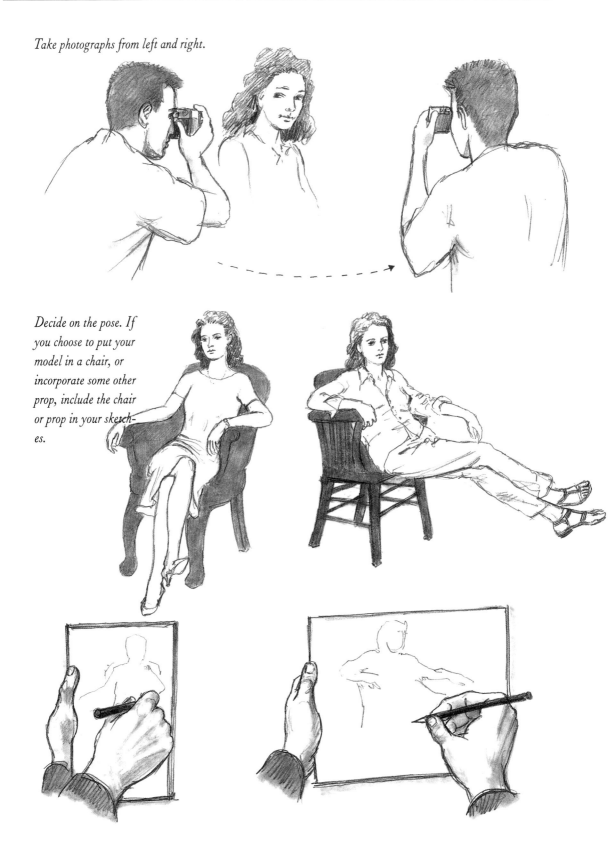

Take photographs from left and right.

Decide on the pose. If you choose to put your model in a chair, or incorporate some other prop, include the chair or prop in your sketches.

What sort of clothing? Casual, formal, tex- tured, patterned or plain? For ideas, see the section on Dress, pages 124–39.

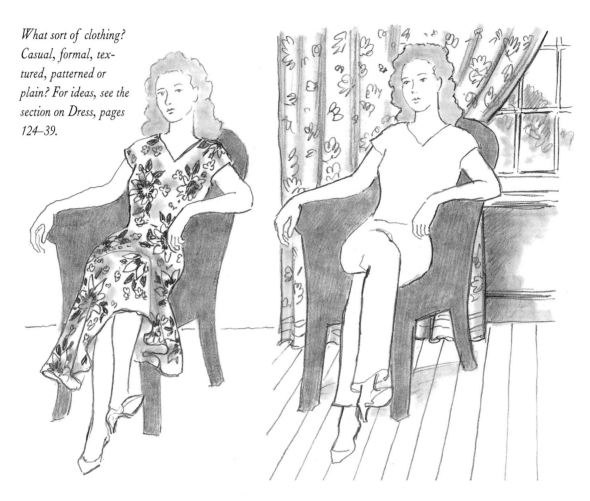

Decide on the lighting: gentle or dramatic? See pages 40–41 for guidance on how to achieve different types of lighting and their effects

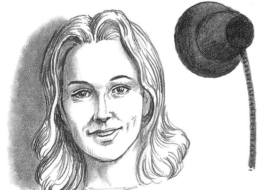
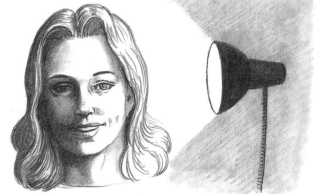

Plan the background. This can be merely a pleasant backdrop or it can be part of the visual narrative and tell the viewer about the sitter. It can be as simple or detailed as you decide to make it. See pages 72–79.

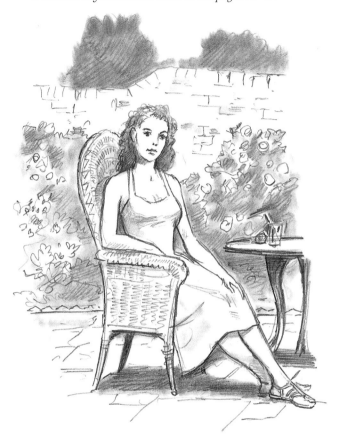

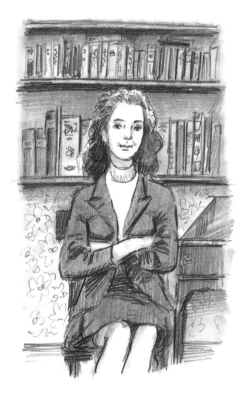

Consider the characteristics of the key features: eyes, mouth and nose. See pages 24–25.

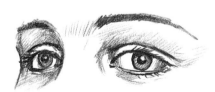

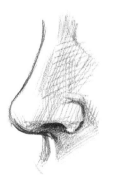

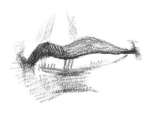

Lighting Your Subject

Any portrait can be affected by the sort of lighting used, whether natural or artificial. Natural lighting is usually the softer of the two types and is the better if you want to see every detail of the face. However, this can have its downside, especially if you want to draw a sympathetic portrait and not highlight the sitter's defects.

Leonardo said that the ideal set up was in a sunlit courtyard with a muslin sheet suspended above the sitter to filter the daylight and give a diffused light. This type of arrangement will be beyond most of us. However, we can aim to get a similar effect with a cool,

diffused light through a large north-facing window.

The artist Ingres described the classical mode of lighting as, 'illuminating the model from an almost frontal direction, slightly to above and slightly to the side of the model's head.' This approach has great merit, especially for beginners in portraiture, because it gives a clear view of the face, but also allows you to see the modelling along the side of the head and the nose, so that the features show up clearly.

Artificial lighting is, of course, extremely flexible, because you can control the direction and amount of light possible and are not dependent on the vagaries of

The light coming from precisely side on produces a dramatic effect, with strong, well marked shadows to the left giving a sharp-edged effect to the shadowed area.

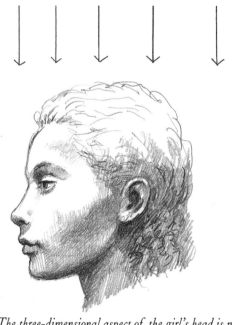

The three-dimensional aspect of the girl's head is made very obvious by lighting coming from directly above, although the whole effect is softer than in the previous example. The shadows define the eyebrows, cheekbones and gently soften the chin and lower areas of the head.

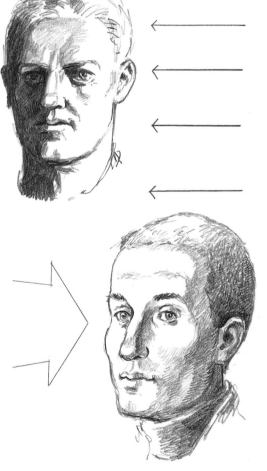

Lighting the face from the front and to one side (as advocated by Ingres) gives a very even set of shadows – in this example on the right side – and clearly shows the bone structure.

the weather. You don't have to invest in expensive equipment to achieve satisfactory results: several anglepoise lamps and large white sheets of paper to reflect light will do very nicely.

Lighting from behind the subject has to be handled very carefully and while it can produce very subtle shadows there is a danger of ending up with a silhouette if the light is too strong. Usually some sort of reflection from another direction creates more interesting definitions of the forms.

The only directional lighting that is not very useful is lighting from beneath the face, because light from below makes the face unrecognizable, which rather defeats the point of a portrait.

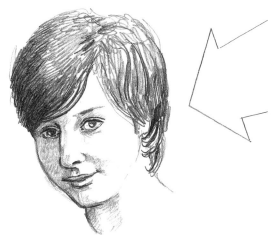

Lit frontally and from above this example also owes a debt to Ingres. The slight tilt of the head allows the shadows to spread softly across the far side of the face.

Lighting the model from directly in front shows the features strongly, subsuming the areas of the hair and the back of the head in deep shadow.

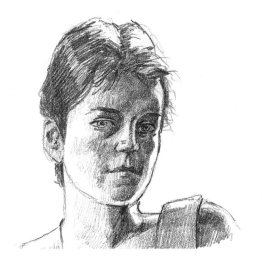

Lighting from behind is not usual in portraiture although it has been done quite effectively. The trick is not to over-do it and end up with your subject in silhouette.

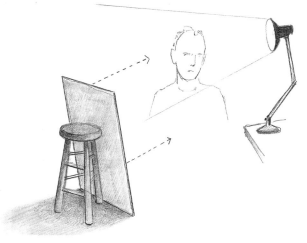

Reflected light can be used to flatten out too many shadows cast over the face. If you want to try this, place a large white sheet of card or similar opposite your light source.

Materials

Any medium is valid for drawing portraits. That said, some media are more valid than others in particular circumstances, and in the main their suitability depends on what you are trying to achieve. Try to equip yourself with the best materials you can afford; quality does make a difference. You don't need to buy all the items listed below, and it is probably wise to experiment gradually, as you gain in confidence. Start with the range of pencils suggested, and when you feel you would like to try something different, then do so. Be aware that each material has its own identity, and you have to become acquainted with its qualities before you can get the best out of it or, indeed, discover whether it is the right material for your purposes. So, don't be too ambitious to begin with, and when you do decide to experiment, persevere.

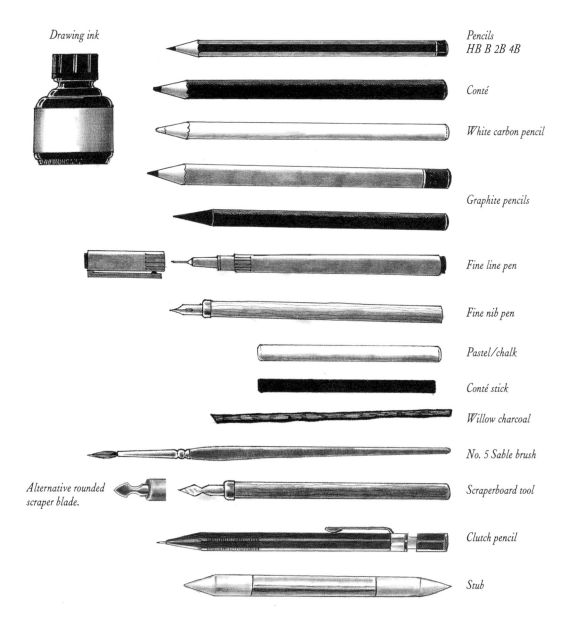

Drawing ink

Pencils
HB B 2B 4B

Conté

White carbon pencil

Graphite pencils

Fine line pen

Fine nib pen

Pastel/chalk

Conté stick

Willow charcoal

No. 5 Sable brush

Alternative rounded scraper blade.

Scraperboard tool

Clutch pencil

Stub

Pencil

The normal type of wooden cased drawing pencil is, of course, the most versatile instrument at your disposal. You will find the soft black pencils are best. Mostly I use B, 2B, 4B and 6B. Very soft pencils (7B–9B) can be useful sometimes and harder ones (H) very occasionally. Propelling or clutch pencils are very popular, although if you choose this type you will need to buy a selection of soft, black leads with which to replenish them.

Conté

Similar to compressed charcoal, conté crayon comes in different colours, different forms (stick or encased in wood like a pencil) and in different grades, from soft to hard. Like charcoal, it smudges easily but is much stronger in its effect and more difficult to remove.

Carbon Pencil

This can give a very attractive, slightly unusual result, especially the dark brown or sepia, and the terracotta or sanguine versions. The black version is almost the same in appearance as charcoal, but doesn't offer the same rubbing out facility. If you are using this type, start off very lightly because you will not easily be able to erase your strokes.

Graphite

Graphite pencils are thicker than ordinary pencils and come in an ordinary wooden casing or as solid graphite sticks with a thin plastic covering. The graphite in the plastic coating is thicker, more solid and lasts longer, but the wooden casing probably feels better. The solid stick is very versatile because of the actual breadth of the drawing edge, enabling you to draw a line a quarter of an inch thick, or even thicker, and also very fine lines. Graphite also comes in various grades, from hard to very soft and black.

Pen

Push-pens or dip-pens come with a fine pointed nib, either stiff or flexible, depending on what you wish to achieve. Modern fine-pointed graphic pens are easier to use and less messy but not as versatile, producing a line of unvarying thickness. Try both types.

The ink for dip-pens is black 'Indian ink' or drawing ink; this can be permanent or water-soluble. The latter allows greater subtlety of tone.

Pastel/Chalk

If you want to introduce colour into your portrait drawing, either of these can be used. Dark colours are best because they give better tonal variation. Avoid bright, light colours. Your choice of paper is essential to a good outcome with these materials. Don't use a paper that is too smooth, otherwise the deposit of pastel or chalk will tend to skid off and not adhere to the paper properly. A tinted paper can be ideal, because it enables you to use light and dark tones to bring an extra dimension to your drawing.

Charcoal

In stick form this medium is very useful for large drawings, because the long edge can be used as well as the point. Charcoal pencils (available in black, grey and white) are not as messy to use as the sticks but are less versatile. If charcoal drawings are to be kept in good condition the charcoal must be fixed with a spray-on fixative to stop it smudging.

Brush

Drawing with a brush will give a greater variety of tonal possibilities to your drawing. A fine tip is not easy to use initially, and you will need to practise if you are to get a good result with it. Use a soluble ink, which will give you a range of attractive tones.

A number 0 or number 2 nylon brush is satisfactory for drawing. For applying washes of tone, a number 6 or number 10 brush in sablette, sable or any other material capable of producing a good point, is recommended.

Scraperboard

The business side of both the black and white versions of scraperboard is covered with a layer of china-clay. The black version has a thin layer of black ink printed evenly over the whole surface which can then be scraped away to produce a reverse drawing resembling a woodcut or engraving. White scraperboard is more versatile, allowing you to apply ink which is then scraped with a sharp point or edge when it is dry to produce interesting textures or lines

Stub

A stub is a tightly concentrated roll of absorbent paper formed into a fat pencil-like shape. Artists use it to smudge marks made with pencil, pastel or charcoal and thus smooth out shading they have applied and graduate it more finely. It is quite a useful tool if you draw a great deal.

Paper

You will find a good-quality cartridge paper most useful, but choose one that is not too smooth; 160gm weight is about right. (If you are unsure, ask in your local art shop, where they will stock all the materials you require.)

Drawing in ink can be done on smoother paper, but even here a textured paper can give a livelier result in the drawing. For drawing with a brush, you will need a paper that will not buckle when wet, such as watercolour paper.

Also see Pastel/Chalk.

Eraser

The best all-purpose eraser for the artist is a putty rubber. Kneadable, it can be formed into a point or edge to rub out all forms of pencil. Unlike the conventional eraser it does not leave small deposits on the paper. However, a standard soft rubber is quite useful as well, because you can work over marks with it more vigorously than you can with a putty rubber.

Most artists try to use an eraser as little as possible, and in fact it only really comes into its own when you are drawing for publication, which requires that you get rid of superfluous lines. Normally you can safely ignore erasers in the knowledge that inaccurate lines will be drawn over and thus passed over by the eye which will see and follow the corrected lines.

Sharpener

A craft knife is more flexible than an all-purpose sharpener and will be able to cope with any thickness of lead or charcoal, etc. It goes without saying that you should always take great care when using such an implement and not leave the blade exposed where it may cause harm or damage.

Styles and Techniques

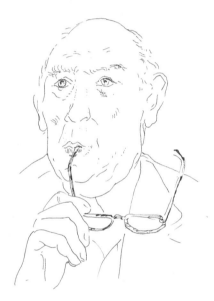

*T*HE PURPOSE OF THIS SECTION is to show you some of the basic techniques that you will need to be able to execute easily and effectively if you are to express the shapes, tones and proportions of what you see. In particular, the practice of the movements of the hand relative to the medium you are using is fundamental to developing a familiarity with your drawing implements. All the methods shown have been used for many years in many ways with lots of local variation. They will add confidence to your mark-making and, as long as they don't become mechanical, should greatly help you to project your intentions.

The way to develop skill in techniques is, of course, by constant practice and drawing every day. By adopting this approach, there is no limit to what you can learn or how much you can improve as an artist. Your technical dexterity should refine over time to make drawing easier and the end result more effective. You have to experiment with new ways of drawing to increase and expand your range of ability. Most student artists like to find out about the techniques other artists have used in order to improve their own expertise, but the acquisition of such skills alone doesn't necessarily produce better drawings. Techniques are only tools to improve your work and should not be used as means to artificially impose a style on it.

Style develops with your skill, but until you have worked through a few different techniques your style doesn't matter much. A natural style evolves as you grow more skilful. Over time this may change or at least vary. Your technical expertise gives you the ability to alter your style to whatever your aims dictate. You become the master of the technique, while your desire for different styles of drawing can develop the necessary range of expression.

As you progress you will absorb many lessons and ideas, and as long as you don't force them they will feed naturally into what you produce. The development of an individual style is a very slow, personal process. Explore, experiment with and practice techniques, but don't expect them to provide an answer. You have to find that for yourself.

Effects with Technique

There are various ways of producing an effective picture by varying the technique you use. Here are a few variations in the treatment of the head of a young man to show you some of the stylistic possibilities.

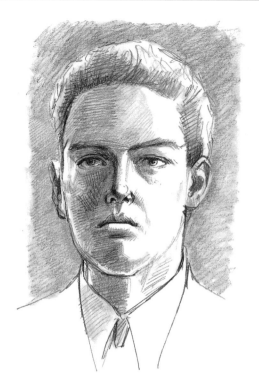

The tones have been worked over with a stub, smudging the pencil to produce a softer, more gradual tonal effect on the areas of shadow. This approach requires fairly vigorous handling of the pencil and the production of strong lines to ensure that the smudging is effective.

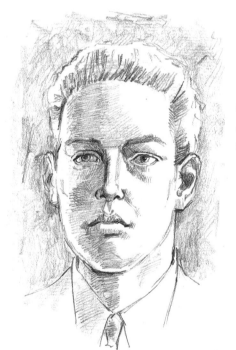

Two grades of pencil (B and 2B) have been used to create texture within the tone. The softer tonal areas, such as the background and hair, were achieved by means of a graphite pencil stick.

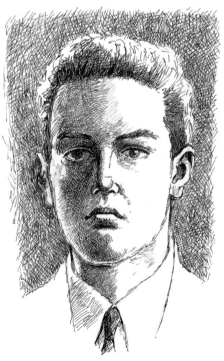

The method used here, in ink, is time-consuming. The tonal areas have been carefully built up with different kinds of cross-hatching and random strokes, giving a solid feel to the head and allowing an exploratory approach to the shape and form.

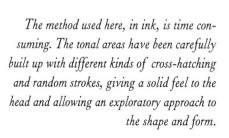

Using a brush and ink or watercolour in one colour will give a painterly feel to your portrait. When attempting this approach, don't be too exact with your brush-strokes. Build up the outlines with fairly loose strokes and then fill in the large areas of tone, initially with very pale washes and then with darker washes.

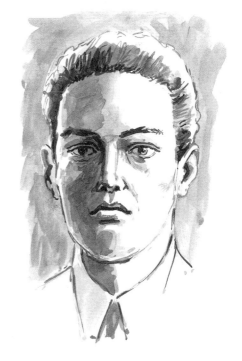

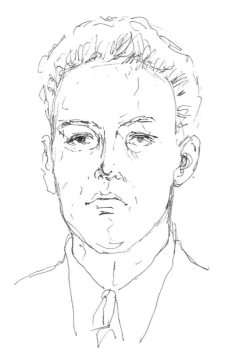

There has been no attempt to build up tone in this example in ink. Open and loosely drawn, it is a very rapid method requiring confidence and facility with the pen. You need to feel your way with your strokes and, as with the previous example, resist the temptation to be too precise.

Up to this point the examples given have been explorations of what you see. This next method is all about using technique to capture form, not likeness. For this approach the initial drawing of the shapes of the head and features has to be very accurate, otherwise the simplification and smoothing out that is the essence of this method will render the final result a bit too perfect in form. You may find that your first swift drawing has captured more of a likeness of the sitter than has your finished drawing. Once you have got the features and tonal areas down, you begin the technical exercise of making the outlines very smooth and continuous so there are no breaks in the line. Then, with a stub, work on the tonal areas until they grade very smoothly across the surface and are as perfect in variation and as carefully outlined as it is possible to make them.

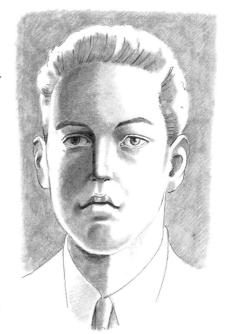

Exercises in Technique

The following technical practices should help you to ease your way into drawing in a range of different styles. There are, of course, many more than the ones we show, but these will serve very well as a basis. You will discover all sorts of other methods through your own investigations and adapt them to serve your purpose.

Pencil Shading Test

When you are using pencil to add tone to your drawings it soon shows if you are not very expert. The only way you can develop this facility is to practise shading in various ways in order to get used to seeing the different tones achievable. This exercise is quite difficult but good fun and can be repeated many times over a period of weeks, just to help you get your hand and eye in. You will find the control it gives you over the pencil very valuable.

You will need a very dark pencil (4B), a slightly less dark pencil (2B) and a lighter pencil (such as a B). If you wish, you can always use a harder lighter pencil, such as an H or 2H.

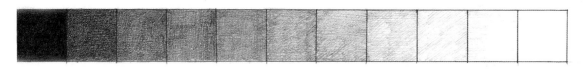

Draw out a long line of squares about 1in (2.5cm) square. Shade each square, starting with a totally black square. Allow the next square of shading to be slightly lighter, and so on, gradually shading each square as uniformly as possible with a lighter and lighter touch, until you arrive at white paper.

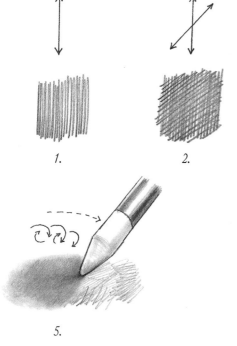

1.   *2.*   *3.*   *4.*

5.

Building up tones by crosshatching:

1. Vertical strokes first, close together

2. Horizontal strokes over the vertical strokes

3. Oblique strokes from top right to bottom left over the strokes shown in 1 and 2.

4. Then make oblique strokes from top left to bottom right over the strokes shown in 1–3.

5. Smooth and finely graduated tones can be achieved by working over your marks with a stub.

Pencil and Graphite

A pencil is the easiest and most obvious implement with which to start an exploration of technique. Try the following series of simple warming up exercises. They can be practised every day that you put aside time to draw. This practice is very useful for improving your technique.

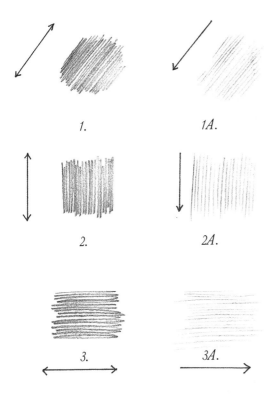

1.

1A.

2.

2A.

3.

3A.

1. *A backward and forward motion of the hand, always in an oblique direction, produces an even tone quickly.*

2. *The same motion vertically.*

3. *The same motion horizontally.*

1A. 2A. and 3A.
Now try a slightly more careful method where the hand draws the lines in one direction only.

Try using a graphite stick for the next two exercises; they can also be done with a well-sharpened soft pencil.

1. *Lay the side edge of the point of the graphite or pencil onto the paper and make smooth, smudged marks.*

2. *Using the point as well in random directions works well.*

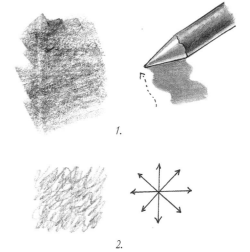

1.

2.

Pen and Ink

There is a whole range of exercises for pen work but of course this implement has to be used rather more lightly and carefully than the pencil so that its point doesn't catch in the paper.

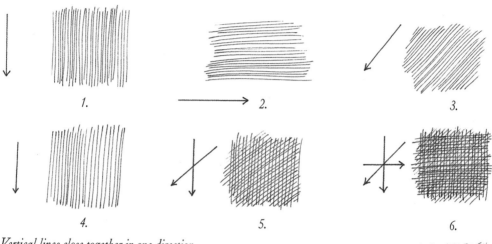

1. Vertical lines close together in one direction.
2. Horizontal lines close together in one direction.
3. Oblique lines close together in one direction.
   Repeat as above but this time building up the strokes:
4. Draw vertical lines.
5. Draw oblique lines on top of the verticals.
6. Draw horizontal lines on top of the oblique and vertical lines.
7. Draw oblique lines at 90 degrees to the last oblique lines on top of the three previous exercises to build up the tone.

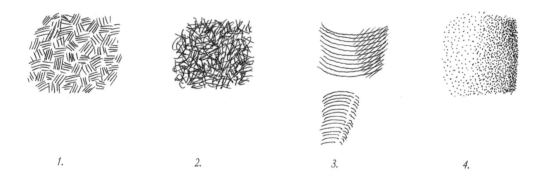

1. Make patches of short strokes in different directions, each time packing them closer together.

2. Draw small overlapping lines in all directions.

3. Draw lines that follow the contours of a shape, placing them close together. For an additional variation, draw oblique lines across these contour lines.

4. Build up myriads of dots to describe tonal areas.

Shading with Chalk

This next series of exercises is similar to the one you have just done but requires extra care not to smudge your marks as you put them down. The key in this respect is not to use a smooth paper. Choose one with a texture that will provide a surface to which the chalk can adhere.

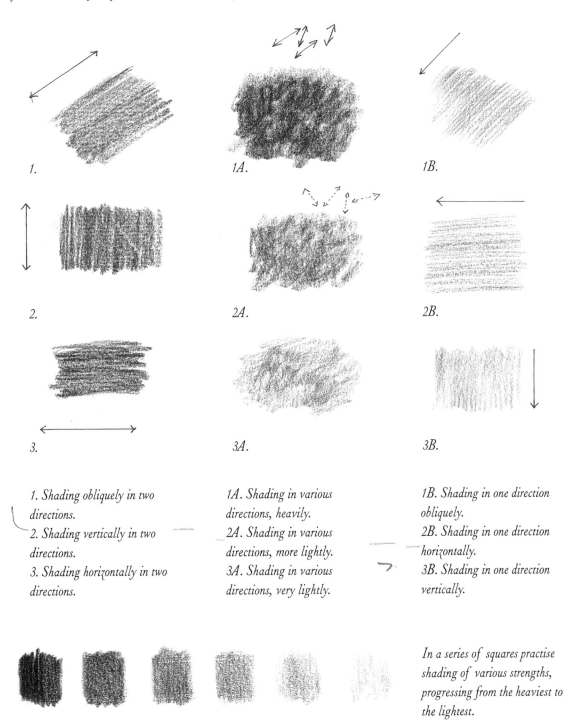

1.

1A.

1B.

2.

2A.

2B.

3.

3A.

3B.

1. Shading obliquely in two directions.
2. Shading vertically in two directions.
3. Shading horizontally in two directions.

1A. Shading in various directions, heavily.
2A. Shading in various directions, more lightly.
3A. Shading in various directions, very lightly.

1B. Shading in one direction obliquely.
2B. Shading in one direction horizontally.
3B. Shading in one direction vertically.

In a series of squares practise shading of various strengths, progressing from the heaviest to the lightest.

Brush and Wash

The best way to start with brush and wash is to try these simple exercises. Your brush should be fairly full of water and colour, so mix a generous amount on a palette or saucer first, and use paper that won't buckle.

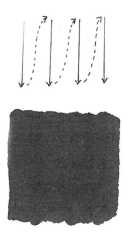

1. With a brush full of ink or watercolour diluted in water, lay a straightforward wash as evenly as possible on watercolour paper.

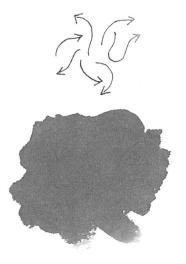

2. Repeat but this time brushing the wash in all directions.

3. Load a lot of colour onto your brush and then gradually add water so that the tone gets weaker as you work. Keep working with the brush until it finally dries and you wipe out the last bit of colour.

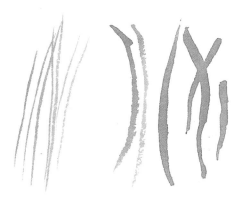

4. Practise drawing soft lines with a brush and wash.

Scraperboard

Take a fine pointed and a curved edge scraper and try your hand at scraperboard. The curved edge tool produces broader, thicker lines than the pointed tool, as can be seen from the examples shown below.

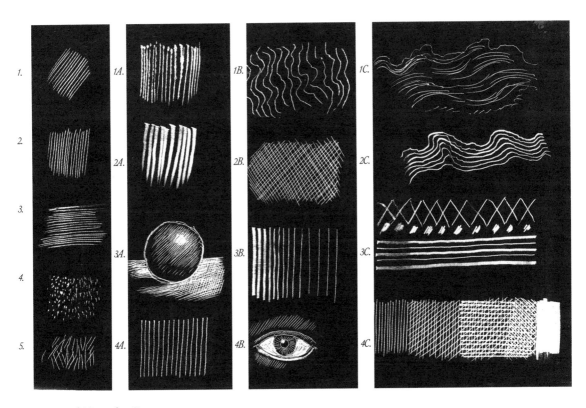

1. Oblique fine line
2. Vertical fine line
3. Horizontal fine line
4. Short pecks
5. Short pecks and strokes
1A. Thicker vertical lines
2A. Thicker oblique lines
3A. Draw a ball, then scrape away to reveal lighter side
4A. Thicker, measured vertical strokes

1B. Scraped wavy lines
2B. Crosshatching with fine lines
3B. Gradually reducing from thick to fine lines
4B. Draw eye shape and then scrape out light areas
1C. Lightly scraped wavy lines
2C. Thickly scraped wavy lines
3C. Criss-cross pattern
4C. Multiple cross-hatching increasing in complexity from left to right

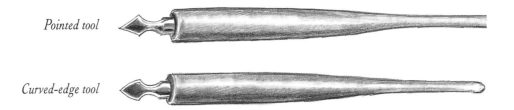

Pointed tool

Curved-edge tool

The Application of Technique

Any technique can be learned, as you will know from the set of technical exercises you have just completed. The test, though, comes in applying technique so that it does not take over your observational faculties or become a strait-jacket.

We are now going to look in detail at a selection of drawings in a range of styles using a range of media and incorporating many of the methods shown in the exercises. In all these examples note how the technique or style is the servant of the artist and his vision.

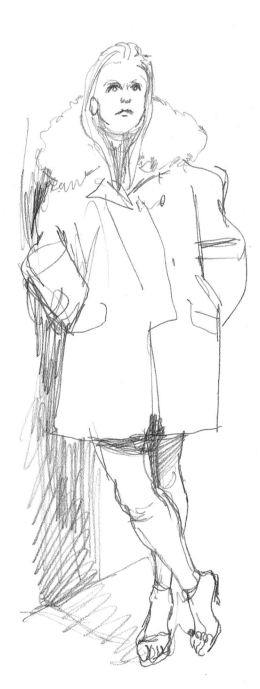

In this pencil drawing the line appears to wander at will to gradual produce an image that is both immediate and relaxed. The pose seems right for this particular method of drawing, looking casual and temporary. Drawing like this can be easily adapted by any artist when they have gained confidence in their ability to see and get the main shapes right. The rather exploratory feel of the wobbly line is very much used by art students as they gain in skill. It has both charm and a certain realism that allows mistakes to be corrected as the line develops without too much difficulty. It is also relatively quick as a method.

Pencil

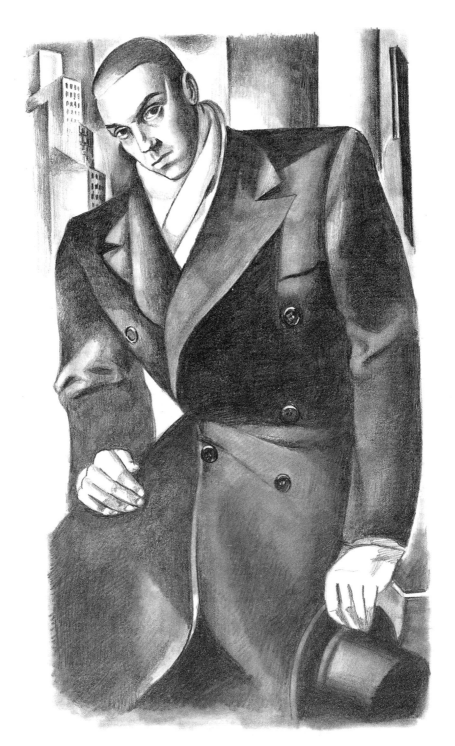

The approach of Tamara de Lempicka in both drawings and paintings was very stylized. In this copy of a portrait of her husband, Tadeusz, the sharp edges of the main shapes have to be put in quite accurately but very smooth-ly, easing out any small bumps and dents. The tones are put in mostly in large areas without much concern for small details. The end result is a solid looking, simplified drawing.

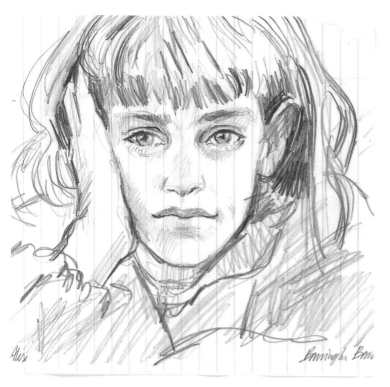

You don't need first-rate materials to produce an effective portrait, as this next example proves. Although I would always advise you to buy the best you can afford, don't make their absence a reason for not drawing something that catches your imagination. I was on a train journey with my family when I had an impulse to draw my youngest daughter. After borrowing a leaf from my wife's notebook and a battered old soft pencil from my daughter it took me about fifteen minutes to complete her portrait. The motion of the train prevented subtlety, forcing me to use slashing strokes. As a result the texture is quite strong, mitigated only by the few softer marks for the tonal areas around the eyes, nose and chin.

Another example using toned paper, this time with a 2B pencil that was not particularly sharp. I opted for the simplest exposition of form and let the paper provide much of the medium tone. After putting in the strongest dark tones I added a few in-between tones, particularly on the hair, and left it at that. The entire portrait took about six minutes. This sort of spontaneous drawing works best if you can see what you want to achieve in one glance and then put it down immediately without deliberation. The result may not be ideal, but taking a chance is what this kind of drawing is all about. It is akin to taking a snapshot with a camera. Practising drawing spontaneous portraits will increase your expertise enormously.

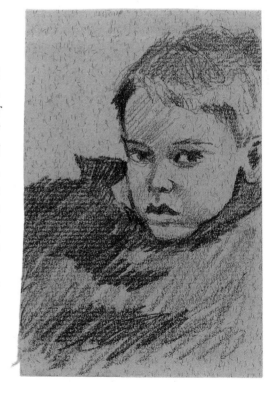

The details of the face are simplified and most of the tonal values dispensed with in this copy of a drawing of Aristide Maillol by fellow sculptor Eric Gill. The different emphasis in the outlines helps to give an effect of dimension, but it is more like the dimension of a bas-relief sculpture, which is perhaps what this study in pencil and stub was about.

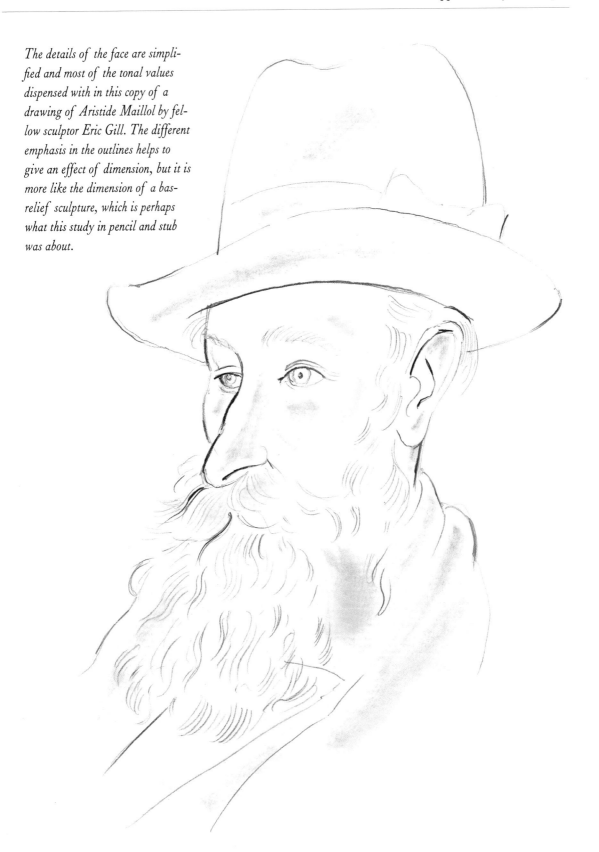

Pen and Ink

*Pen and ink is ideal for producing mini-
malist yet revealing studies, such as this
copy of a David Hockney drawing of
Sir Isiah Berlin. The spare lines, broken
and tentative, are carefully placed to get
the shape and
character of the features.
Each line is a one-off chance,
perfectly judged so as not to
overweight the surface, as
some artists might do.*

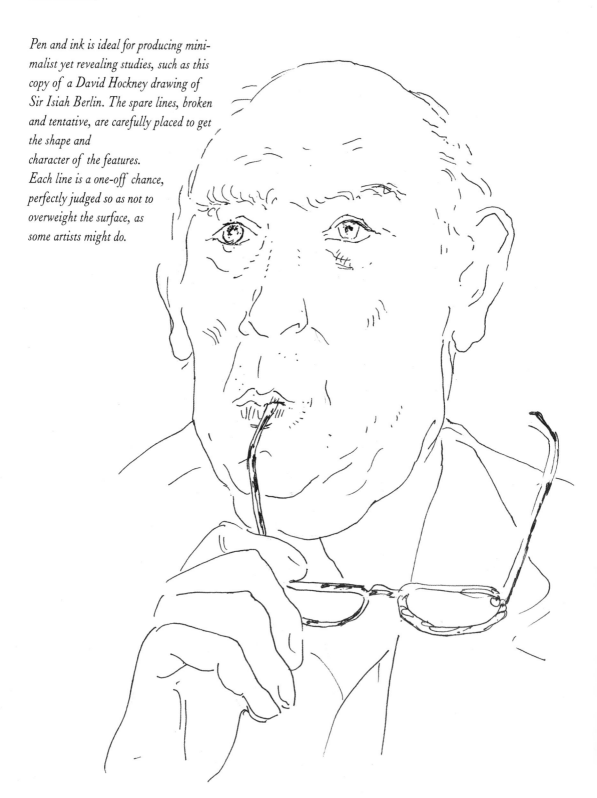

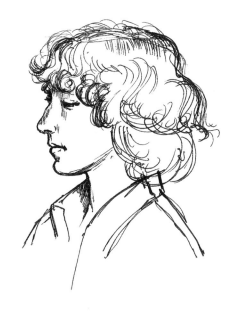

The most time-consuming aspect of this pen and ink drawing (fountain pen with a fine point on fairly thin paper) was tracing out the profile. The drawing had to be done quickly because the model was only available for a few minutes, being part of a class of art students sitting for one another. The outline was the main point of emphasis, with a bit of tone, especially on the hair. It is important with quick drawings to concentrate on one aspect and not try to be too clever.

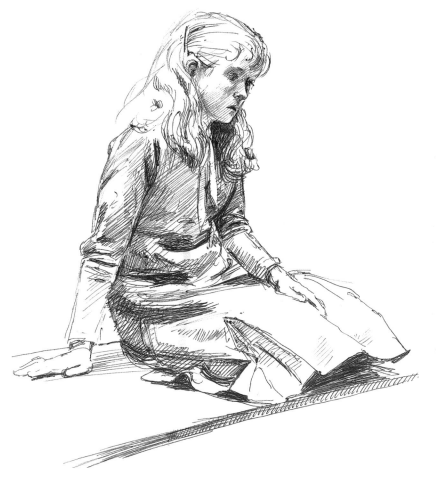

An ordinary fountain pen with a fine nib was used to produce this quick sketch. The technique is almost scribbly because, as with the first example, only a few minutes were available to get the drawing down. The tonal areas had to be put in very simply with the dark areas gone over repeatedly to give them sufficient emphasis. The contrast between the dark areas and the uncovered areas is important for the final feeling of dimension in the drawing.

Chalk

Chalk always gives a soft, attractive finish and is very popular for portraits, although you need to keep your drawing as clean as possible, otherwise you are liable to end up with a mass of smudges. Chalk makes a mark whether or not you press, so it is important to keep your touch light.

In this copy of a David Hockney, the eyes say it all. The other features are rendered very simply, almost as outlines. The texture of the hair serves to give an impression of the shape of the head. The key to Hockney's brilliant minimalist style is sound judgement of emphasis: nothing is overworked.

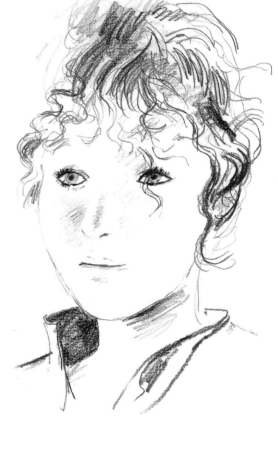

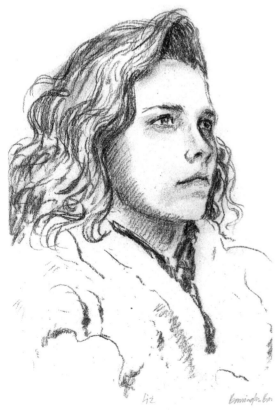

This black chalk drawing on a tinted paper took about twenty minutes. The style is fairly simple and the technique quite easy. The face has been drawn in without much modelling and with the emphasis on placing the features correctly. Interest has been created by the texture of the chalk line and the model's attractive longish hair.

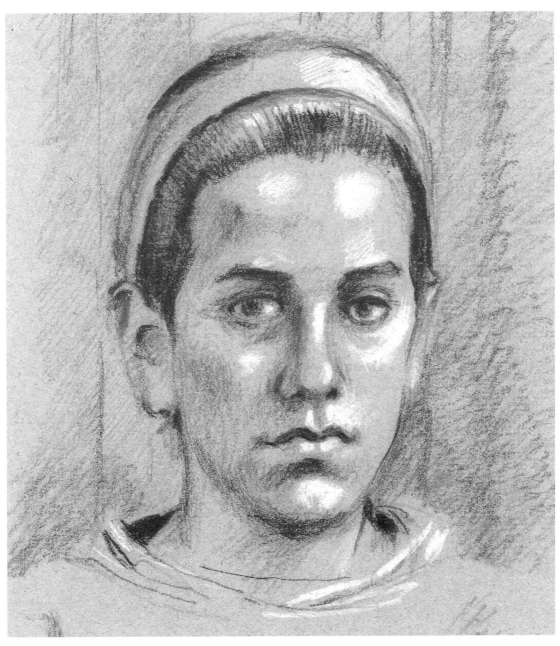

The most dimension is achieved for the least effort in this example. The reason is the use of three materials in combination: brown and terracotta conté pencil, white chalk and toned paper. These give such a range of tones that they obviate the need to work a drawing too heavily. Notice how the strong emphasis provided by the darker of the conté pencils is kept to a minimum, sufficient to describe what is there but no more. Similarly the chalk is used only for the strongest highlights. The mid-tone is applied very softly, with no area emphasized over-much. The toned paper is a great asset and does much of the artist's work, enabling rapid production of a drawing but one with all the qualities of a detailed study. Often you will find it effective to include some background to set off the lighter side of the head, which in this example is the right side as we look at it.

Brush and Wash

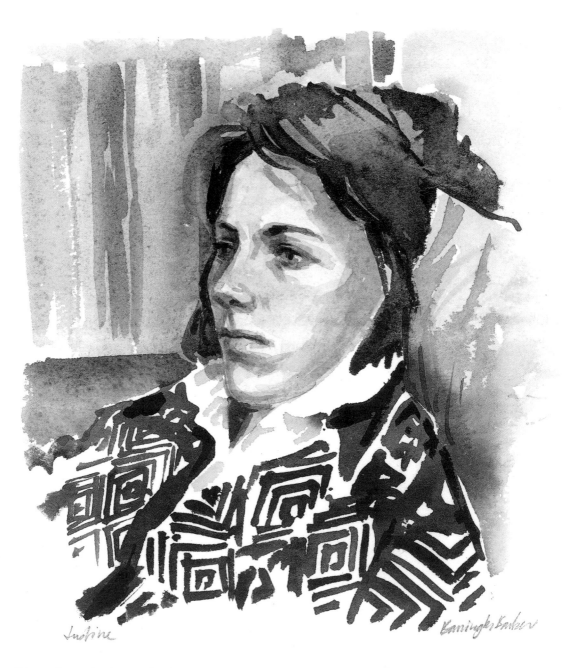

Plenty of water has been used to keep the tones on the face and the background soft in this example of watercolour on watercolour paper. The strength of colour on the jacket and hair is greater than elsewhere in the picture. The eyes, nose and mouth need touches of strong tone, especially the line of the mouth where it opens and the upper eyelashes, eyebrows and pupils of the eyes. This type of drawing can be built up quite satisfactorily, with the lighter tones put in first all over and then strengthened with the darks.

Scraperboard

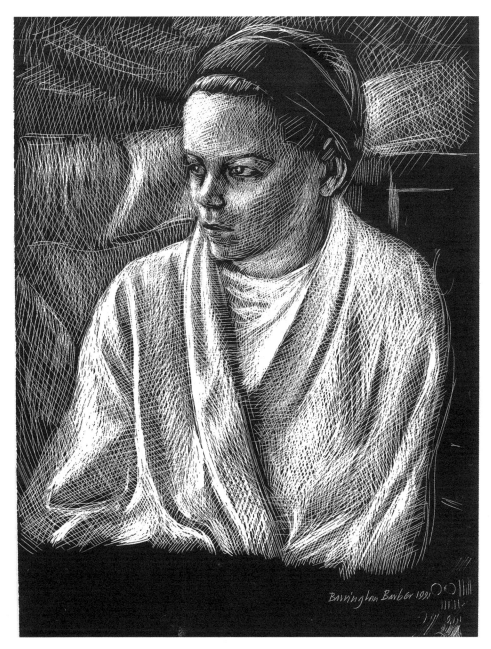

With scraperboard technique the artist has to draw back-to-front, revealing all the light areas and leaving the dark ones. Usually it is the other way round. This subject was ideal for the purpose, her white bath-robe ensuring there were plenty of light areas, although it was difficult to judge how much to work the face. The hair and hairband were made up of dark tones, and so required only the addition of highlights.

Similar effects to scraperboard can be obtained with white chalk on black paper. Try it as an exercise; it will teach you a great deal about gauging the balance of light and dark.

Mixed Media

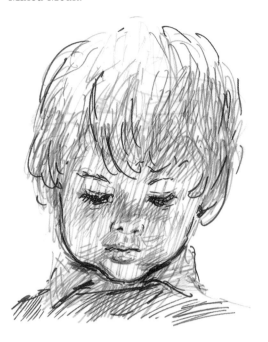

A range of coloured felt-tip pens were used for this spontaneous drawing, hence the variation in tonal effect in the lines. Felt-tip is a fairly coarse medium, so I was careful to leave space between the lines, except in the outline.

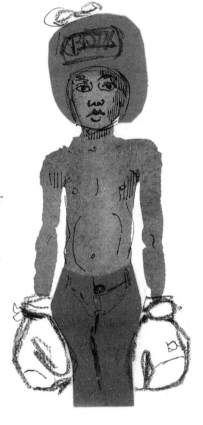

This is a good example of how easy it can be to experiment with a range of different techniques in one picture. The various mediums – which include collage (sticking on paper), pen and ink, wash and brush, and pencil – add interest and colour to what is a simple subject of a young Cuban boy at a boxing training session. The style produces a quick, effective image and shows that you can get results without the need for a highly detailed drawing.

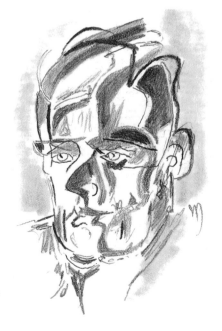

A copy of a portrait of T. S. Eliot the poet by Patrick Heron the artist, who somehow manages to produce a portrait that actually looks like the writer without being at all conventional in approach. Heron uses an almost abstract technique in which he points up certain areas of the features and then draws other features across them. The effect is that of a composite portrait. The profile of nose, mouth and chin is emphasized, and drawn across them are the eyes and full face.

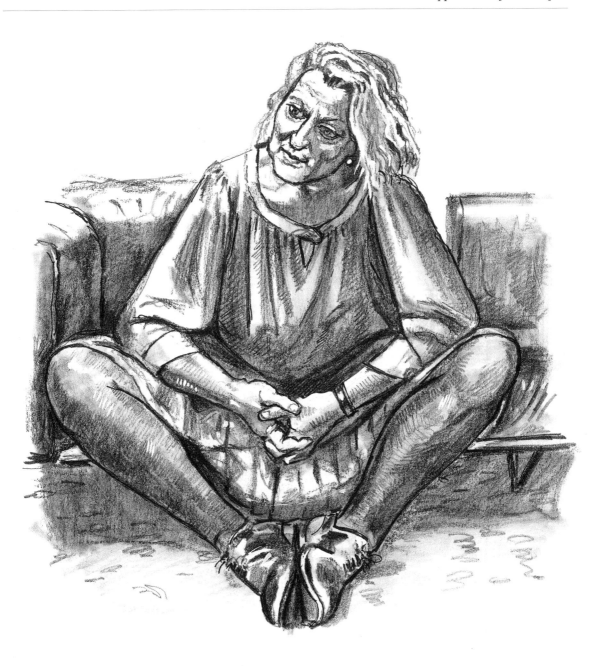

The original of this portrait of academic and writer Germaine Greer by Paula Rego was made in pastel on paper laid on aluminium; this copy is in chalk, pencil and pen and ink. The difficulty of producing a simple black and white copy of coloured pastel is that the slightly coarser medium of the fast-moving pastel has to be reproduced both smaller and finer while retaining the feel of the original. Careful handling of the different mediums is required to make such a copy work so that it does justice to the attributes of the original.

Composition

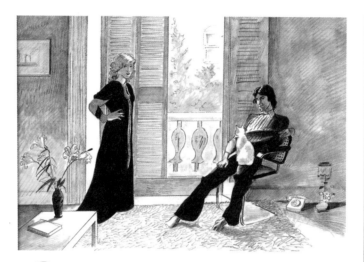

COMPOSING A PICTURE is always important and this is no less true of a portrait than of any landscape, still life, or figure composition. At the beginning you may find that you are literally only drawing faces so that composition hardly comes into it, but as you get more competent it is essential to consider the composition, even if only for a short time.

Even a single head, as large as can be fitted into the paper shape, is a compositional statement. How much space is there around the head? How does the hair relate to the face? Is the background dark or light? These are just some of the questions you have to address when you begin your portrait.

However, if you want to have a deeper, wider space around your head or figure, what must the relationship be between all this background space and the subject? Psychologically this surround or background to the person being portrayed is very useful for giving something of the character, life or profession of the sitter. Some artists will use the setting to tell you something about the sitter; for example by giving clues to their home life, their occupation, their family situation or revealing something which emphasizes an aspect of their character or status.

In the most famous paintings of the high and mighty, the settings are invariably splendid with backgrounds of sumptuous drapes, architectural details or landscapes of imposing grandeur. Sometimes the background is as mysterious as the subject; for example in Leonardo's Mona Lisa, where the beautiful, almost dissolving watery landscape adds depth and mystery to the portrait.

In many 'swagger' portraits the background looks more akin to a stage set than a realistic depiction of architectural or natural details. Such theatrical settings help to portray a public persona rather than a private one and inhabit the realm of propaganda. In some interior portraits articles of furniture will tell us about the status or situation of the sitter, and often include reflections or other pictures which give us clues to the story of the person's life and achievements.

Intelligent consideration of how to set your subject before you put pencil to paper will ensure that you convey far more than a simple representation of that individual.

Placement in the Frame

Once you have chosen a subject to draw the next step is to look at composition. The most basic compositional consideration is how you arrange the figure in the frame of the picture. The pose or attitude you choose will have a large bearing on this. There are many compositional permutations that can be brought to a portrait, as you will quickly discover when you start to look at the work of other artists. Each of the arrangements shown here conveys an idea or mood associated with the subject. Before choosing a composition you must be sure it is right for your purposes. Good composition is never accidental.

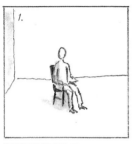
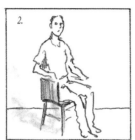
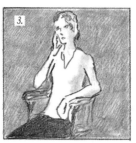
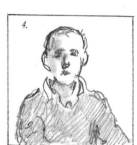

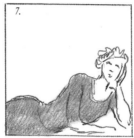
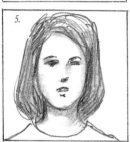
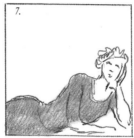
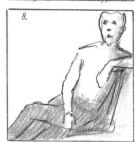

1. This figure is set well back in a room with lots of space around him. In order for the sitter to be clearly recognizable the picture would have to be huge. There would be a reason for choosing this degree of detachment from the viewer.

2–5. In this series of viewpoints the onlooker gets a progressively closer picture of the sitter. Generally longer views give a more detached picture. A tight close up of the head demands that the artist achieve an accurate likeness, both physically and in terms of psychological insight.

6–8. An off-centre position can produce a dramatic, unpredictable effect. The picture becomes more than just a recording of someone's likeness, and we begin to consider it as an aesthetic, artistic experience. The space in the picture acts as a balance to the dynamic qualities of the figure or face. It can also be used to indicate qualities about the sitter, especially if they have a retiring personality.

9. Not many faces can stand such a large, detailed close up and not many people would be comfortable with this approach. However, it is extremely dramatic.

10. In this unusual and interesting arrangement, enough is shown of this figure turning away from the viewer for him to be recognizable.

11. Showing a half figure to one side of the picture with a dark background is a good approach for colourful characters or if you want to add some mystery to a portrait.

12. Firmly placed centre stage in an uncompromising pose

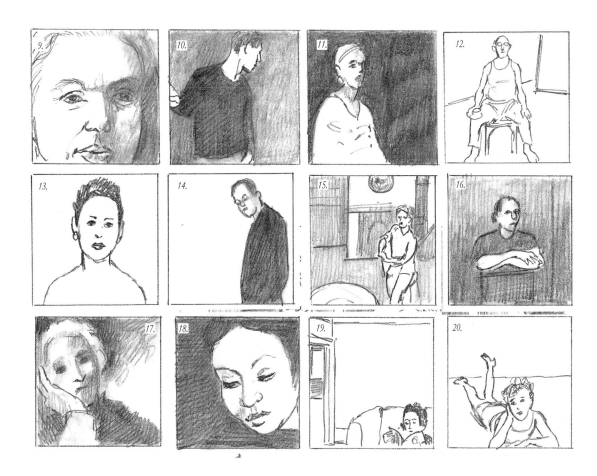

this sitter comes across as very confrontational. The well-lit background and foreground ensure that nothing is left to the imagination, accentuating the no-nonsense direct view of the subject.

13. This head and shoulders view is evenly lit with little or no tonal values and absolutely no decorative effects. As such it demands a very attractive face.

14. The rather indirect positioning of the figure suggests a diffident character, and an almost reluctant sitter.

15. The figure takes up only one quarter of the frame, with most of the space given up to the sitter's domestic surroundings. The emphasis here is on lifestyle and the ambience of home.

16. This sitter is made mysterious and moody by the device of posing him so that he is not looking at the viewer.

17. A soft, slightly out of focus effect can be very flattering, and in this example gives a sympathetic close-up of an elderly woman.

18. This close-up of a face floating in a dark void gives a dream-like effect.

19. An off-beat dramatic twist has been brought to this portrait by placing the sitter at the bottom of the picture, as though she is about to sink from our view.

20. This sitter is presented as playful, almost coquettish, by placing her along the lower half of the picture in a relaxed lying-down pose.

Classic Rules

At one time portrait painting was exclusively the preserve of the well-heeled, the well-connected and the powerful, and for this reason there were very set conventions regarding composition. It went without saying, for example, that a portrait should include devices that pointed up the subject's social standing or worthiness. Over the centuries this would change, but very slowly, and in the meantime people got used to 'reading' paintings and understanding their content through the composition.

The background of a portrait often told the viewer a clear story connected with the subject's lifestyle. The props or clothing as well as the amount of the figure shown, and the style of showing the figure, would be understood in the context of the social life of the period. If a portrait was of a ruler, emperor or king, then the size would be large, the figure would be shown in a decidedly heroic stance and often all the clothing and objects depicted would indicate the power of the sitter. Most leaders would be shown with such objects as maps, legal documents, military headgear etc. to indicate their area of status. However, although there were clearly understood rules of composition, these were always open to radical interpretation. The great artists would re-state or completely change the composition, their powerful aesthetic understanding producing a new way of looking at their society. Once the master had set a new mode of portraiture, lesser artists could quickly follow suit and so whole schools of artists would set the fashion for an age.

The portraits we look at next are examples from historical pictures which in their different ways define the sitter from clearly understood rules of composition. The background is everything seen behind or around the figure but not advanced in front of it. The setting could be anything from furniture to animals or props.

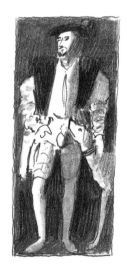

The portrait of Emperor Charles V by Titian leaves us in no doubt as to the sitter's importance and that this man is a leader. The stance and dress give a complete feeling of ease with his role. The background has been left as a dark shadowy space, as if there was no point in trying to define this man's role. Even without background clues, Titian is saying that his society, knowing the unusually powerful role of this monarch and that he is a charismatic and able warrior, will be impressed enough by the man himself. Charles was indeed an unusual ruler and this judgement by Titian was not misunderstood at the time.

This is a copy of a typical ruler's portrait, in this instance of Louis XVI of France. However, although the court painter knew the system of representation for such a figure, his artistry and the character of the monarch are not powerful enough to give us an impressive painting of a great man. The breadth and depth of the scene, with its gorgeous coronation robes and background hangings, and the classical allusions to dignity and status in the architectural details, only serve as scenery for a splendid but empty pageant.

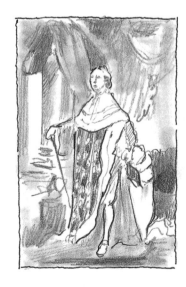

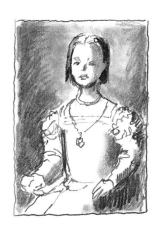

Bronzino has produced a charming piece in his depiction of a young princess, sitting upright as befits her status, and yet still very tenderly portrayed as a favourite child. The background is almost non-existent; we are merely aware of the chair upon which she is formally placed, which almost dwarfs her but at the same time sets her up in a position of potential power.

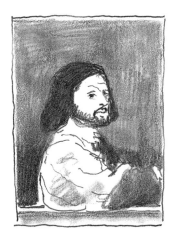

Another Titian masterpiece, of the poet Ariosto, set the fashion for future portraits by showing a simple head and shoulders. The composition convinces us of the importance of the sitter merely by the bravura stance of the pose, plus the extraordinary power in the intelligence of the face. The mere fact of being painted by a great master in itself conferred a degree of importance on a sitter.

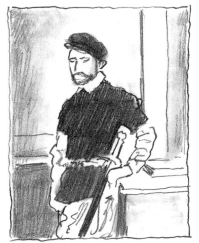

Moroni's portrait of the Duke of Alberqueque shows something of the man's humanity and awkwardness in his pose as a gallant of the Spanish court. The pillar on which he leans is a good classical adjunct to an otherwise bare background wall, which helps to suggest that he is a man of consequence. A full-figure depicted a ruler, a half-figure a less, but still powerful, being and so on down to just a head.

This second Moroni portrait tells us about the nature of the sitter's trade. The customer for this picture was probably a tailor who wanted a composition that said something about his employees. It's very unusual to find portraits of ordinary, working people and there may be a moralistic or didactic motivation behind the picture.

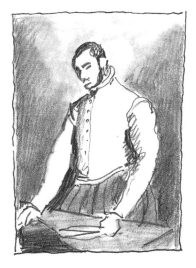

Meaning in Background

Whereas a room can be both a setting and a background, a distant landscape is very much a background feature. In these examples there is a contrast in the use of background, although at first glance you might be forgiven for thinking the idea behind them was very similar.

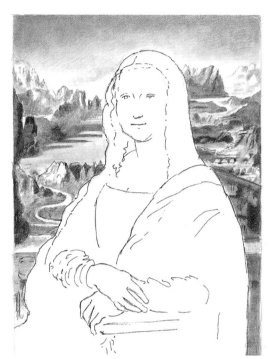

The setting of the Mona Lisa is a puzzle. Why it was thought appropriate to place the wife of a wealthy Florentine merchant in front of such a landscape is not known. Whatever the truth of the matter, the background comprises all the naturalistic features Leonardo was so good at producing in new combinations. It also reinforces the air of mystery that is evoked by this extraordinary portrait, and so validates his reason for choosing it.

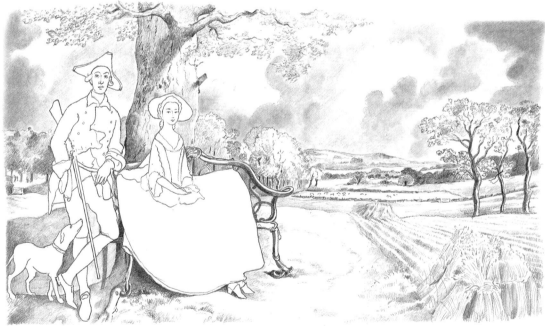

Gainsborough's portrait of Mr and Mrs Andrews is an interesting development of the 'swagger' portrait. The placement of the couple suggests that the landscape may be more the point of this picture than the couple themselves. The Suffolk landscape stretches out on the right side of the composition, bathed in warm sunlight which highlights the clear traces of agricultural activity. Andrews was a forward-thinking landowner, keen to use the latest farming techniques, and to the right we see the marks left by a seed drill, which in the 18th century was a great innovation.

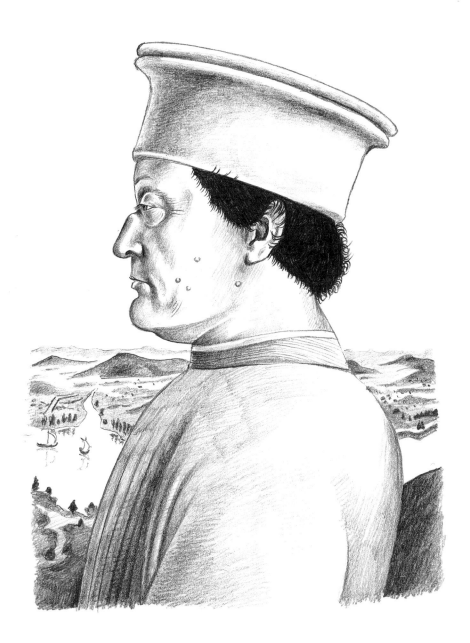

In this copy of *Piero della Francesca's portrait of his friend and patron, Federico da Montefeltro, the background provides a rich context for the subject. Montefeltro, ruler of Urbino, was a famous condottiere, and the ships and fortifications shown along the river are indications of his military prowess. The Duke was also a leading patron of the arts and learning, and in times of peace he occupied himself in the pursuit of Renaissance ideals. The artist presents us with an apparently simple profile which tells us that Federico is benign, powerful and wise. The eyes are far-seeing, fixed on a point beyond our gaze. Also hidden from us is the war wound on the other side of the duke's face. Della Francesca has not, however, hidden his subject's personality. The head sits above the background, with nothing to distract the eye. This is a sympathetic yet revealing portrait of a man who is clearly both a thinker and doer.*

Settings

One of the most difficult aspects of the preliminary stage of producing a portrait is the setting. Quite often you will see the face and features of your subject very clearly and yet have little idea of the sort of background or setting in which to pose them. Sometimes the background that ends up in a portrait is the one that just happened to be behind the person when the artist first drew them. However, that situation is less than ideal. The background is part of the effect you are trying to create, and contributes to the visual and metaphorical picture you are constructing, so it demands your attention and is worth putting a great deal of thought into.

When the whole figure is in the portrait the background and setting become especially important. It may be that you decide to have a blank or empty background behind the head, to ensure that the viewer concentrates solely on the figure. Even a simple background can have dramatic effect; for example, a dark tone behind and around the head can make it project out of the background, whereas a light tone will isolate the head without projecting it forwards.

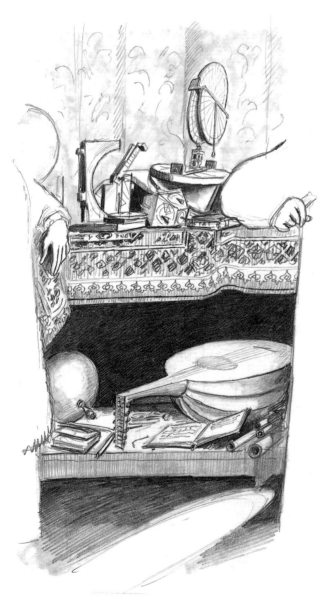

Hans Holbein's 'The French Ambassadors to the English Court' was painted to record the visit of Georges de Selve (a bishop) to his friend Jean de Dinterville in 1533. The setting consists of a two-tier table on which are placed items associated with the interests and affairs of the two men. On the top level are instruments used for mapping the heavens and making calculations of time, date and the movements of the sun, all activities of interest to gentlemen of a humanist persuasion. On the lower shelf we see a lute and a book of Lutheran hymns. The latter says something for the Catholic bishop's pragmatism; as ambassador to the English court and the strongest Protestant nation in Europe at the time, he would have had to show tolerance in matters of religion. The carpet on the upper shelf and the background curtain give evidence of the richness of the household.

Holbein often produced carefully invented settings. For this example, it is very doubtful whether the ambassadors sat for any longer than it took to draw and paint their faces. A servant would probably have stood in for them, and the still-life on the table would have been painted in the studio when the sitters were absent.

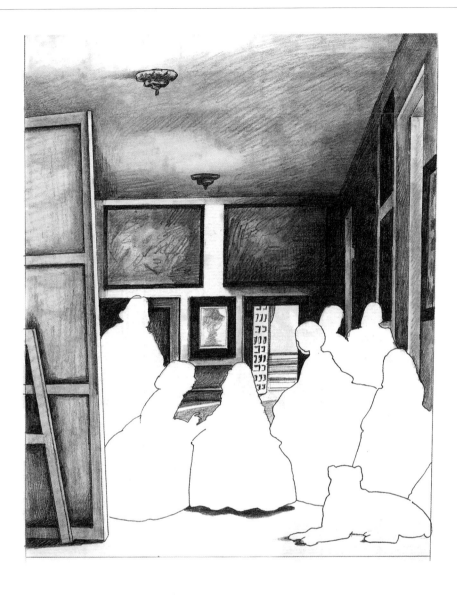

It says a great deal about Velázquez's relationship with his patrons, the Spanish royal family, that they allowed the painter to pose their young daughter in his studio. A tiny figure in the huge space of the studio, she stands at the centre of a lovely informal composition. Around her are her maids (hence the title of the picture, 'Las Meninas'/The Maids of Honour), a dwarf, a large dog and, to the left, a self-portrait of the artist engaged on producing the picture. We see the reverse of a large canvas leaning on an easel. One of the maids is curtseying to figures directly in front of where the viewer stands. In the original, two figures are dimly reflected in the mirror on the wall behind Velázquez and the Infanta, possibly visual references to the child's parents, the king and queen. Hanging in the gloom of the upper walls, we can see paintings.

The scene seems accidental as though it is not intended for our eyes. On the other hand it does offer a window onto the world of the artist, with the viewer becoming a witness to his act of creation and an insider in the artistic process.

Velázquez's brilliant scheme has been much copied by other artists, including Picasso, who based a whole series of works on it.

Playing with Convention

Here we look at examples of composition from two undoubted contemporary masters of portraiture, David Hockney and Lucian Freud. While Hockney has chosen to borrow from past conventions, Freud has more obviously struck out on his own. Both approaches make us either question the situation or provoke our curiosity, either of which is a good response to any portrait.

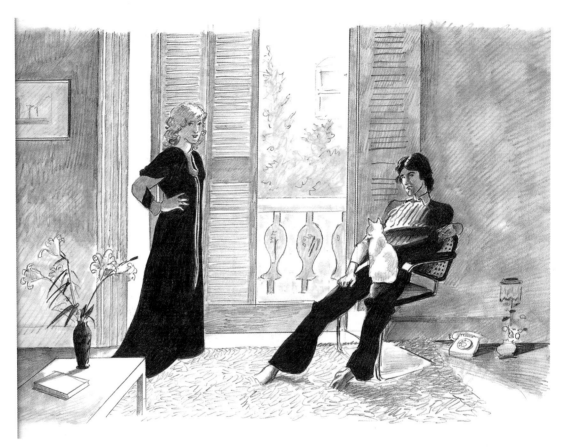

David Hockney's ability to echo the fashionable colour schemes of modern life in his work made him an obvious choice as portraitist of a fashion designer. In this copy, Ossie Clarke and his wife and their cat, Percy, are shown at home in their flat. The positioning of the figures is formal, almost classical, accentuated by the very dark dress of the woman and the dark legs of Clarke himself with Percy, outstanding in white, making three. There is minimal furniture, which might be as it was or because the *artist arranged it that way. The white lilies in the vase on the table could be intended as symbols of purity. Cats were often symbols for lust, so although Percy's colour might qualify him as another icon of purity, tradition suggests otherwise. The position of both flowers and the cat is interesting in relation to the main subjects. The shadowed walls adjacent to the bright slot of the window give both space and a dramatic tonality which contrasts well with the two figures.*

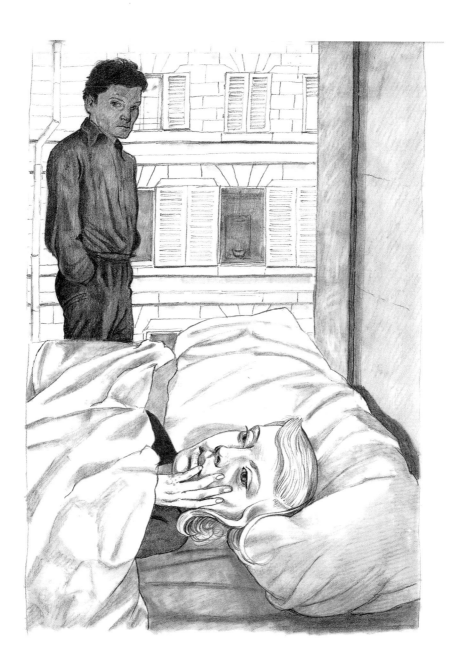

In *Lucian Freud's double portrait of himself and his wife in a Parisian hotel bedroom the poses are as informal as the situation is ambiguous. Why is she in bed and he standing by the window? Obviously he needed to be upright in order to produce the portrait but he hasn't shown us that he is the artist. There is no camera, sketch book or easel and brushes in his hands. So what could be his intention? There is an explanation that Freud's wife was ill in bed at the time, so it may have been that he hit on the arrangement because it was the only way he could paint them both. In the hands of a first-class artist this unusual approach has become a ground-breaking idea. The slightly accidental look of the composition is very much of the period in which it was painted (the 1950s).*

The Influence of Photography

Since the advent of photography the rules of portrait painting have been more or less thrown out of the window, although there is still a kind of institutional portraiture that follows those rules. Nowadays the composition is more a way of surprising the viewer by its novelty, and making its point more as a piece of design technique than a way of reassuring the sitter as to his or her position in life. Nevertheless, there are still clever artists who can imbue their pictures with qualities of beauty, power and characterful figuration associated with the best examples of traditional portraiture.

The two examples featured here exhibit compositional arrangements that would not have been seen in a painting before the advent of photography. Although vastly different in style, both have their conception in a view of presentation that comes directly out of our familiarity with photography.

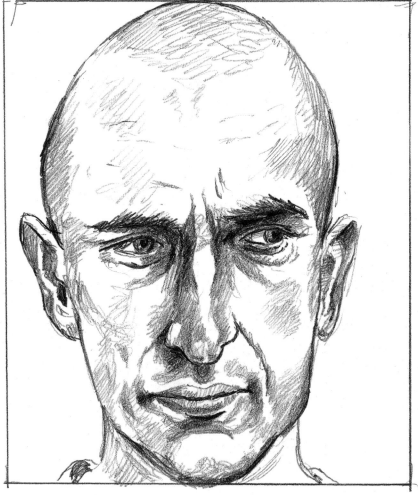

After 'Mug Shot', by Catherine MacDiarmid. The arrangement in the frame has the effect of a badly taken snapshot. The deliberate placing of the head in a sort of limbo has an alienating effect and presents a bleak, albeit powerful, view of the subject.

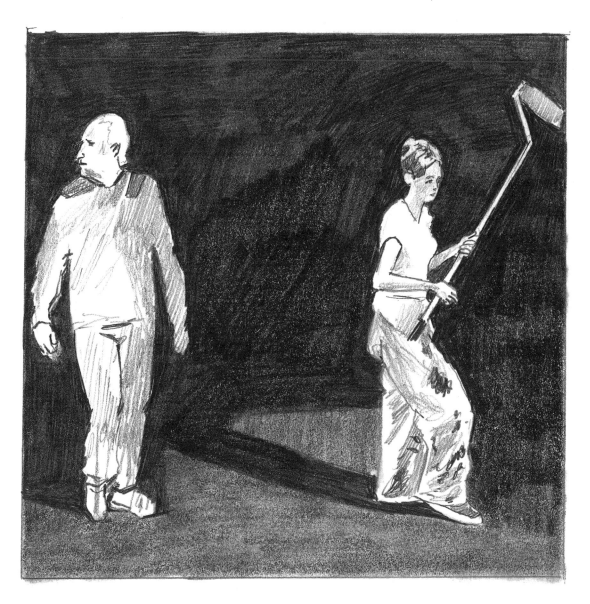

Compositionally this double portrait (after 'Paint It Black' by Sarah McConkey) looks like an example of journalistic photography, reminding us of one of those shots of celebrities momentarily caught by the paparazzi when least wanting to be. The space in the centre and the figures almost off the edge give the effect of movement. The original composition was probably based on a photograph, judging by the tension in the poses.

Posing

When arranging your subject, notice should be taken of the hands, arms and legs because they will make quite a significant impression on the overall composition. Portrait artists have always been interested in the relationship of the limbs because it can make a definite statement about a sitter's character or state of mind.

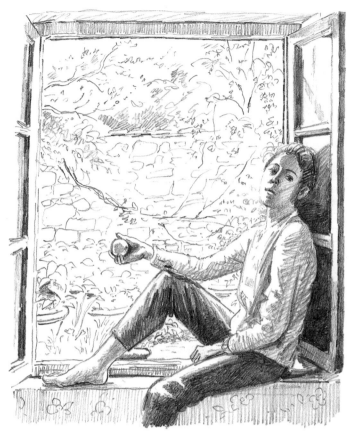

In this seemingly very relaxed portrait the frame of the window is also the frame of the portrait. The angles of the limbs make for a very interesting composition within this frame. It is not an easy pose to hold for any length of time, and so quick sketches and photographs were needed as reference for the final portrait.

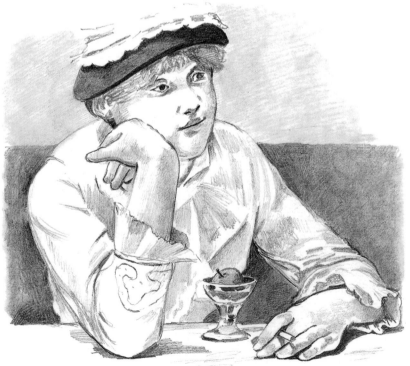

In this copy of a Manet, a young woman is sitting draped around her plum dessert, a cigarette in her left hand while her right hand supports her cheek. The naturalistic pose gives a gentle, relaxed air to the portrait.

Hands

Hands laying in the lap in a passive fashion give an effect of peacefulness and poise. Hands touching the face or hair can bring the attention of the viewer to interesting features of the head, and act rather as a lead-in for the eye. And, of course, by showing hands placed on specific objects in a picture the artist is giving information about the interests, status or profession of the sitter.

This detail is taken from a portrait of Lady Dacre by Hans Eworth. Here the hands tell the viewer not just about the learning of the scholarly lady (note the thumb keeping her place in the book in her left hand), but about her creative ability as she moves to write in her journal. Literary and educational pursuits were becoming fashionable in the 16th century and so these compositional props are very obvious symbols of the sitter's status. If the book she holds is a scriptural work, this would also reflect on the lady's piety, in an age when religion was a serious part of the life of the ruling class.

The hands of the elderly Catholic prelate Cardinal Manning, after a painting by G. F. Watts. The pose is appropriately peaceful and non-aggressive and is similar to one done much earlier by Raphael of the Pope.

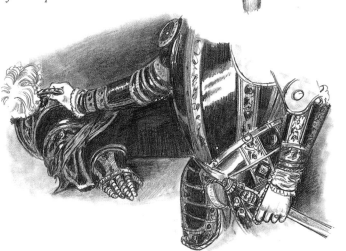

Phillip II of Spain, by Titian, grasps the crest of a helmet while his left hand holds the scabbard of his sword just below the hilt. As he is also in half armour, the inference is clear that this king will not flinch from taking military action to defend and expand his kingdom.

Posing: Arms

Arms often betray a strong attitude that gives the sitter an individual strength. The artist may use the arms to create balance in an off-centre picture, or as a strong statement to reinforce the structure of the position of the sitter.

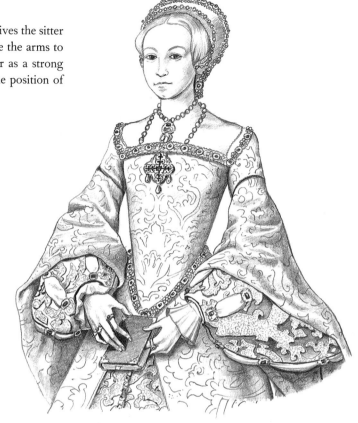

The young Princess Elizabeth before she became England's greatest queen, demurely holding her book with a finger keeping the place where she is studying. She was a good scholar in scripture and languages. The arrangement of the arms in their fashionably ornate sleeves suggests some power in the stance. The direct stare is challenging, and she looks every inch a royal personage. The position of the arms is formal and balanced, which gives strength to her slight figure.

Joshua Reynolds' painting of the dashing Duchess of Devonshire with her little son was in its time a ground-breaking picture. The hands and arms held up in delight and fun by the child in response to the mother's playful gesture was a remarkable novelty in portraiture. The naturalness of the interaction between the subjects stops this being just another fashionable portrait and turns it into a study of the interplay that occurs between any mother and her infant.

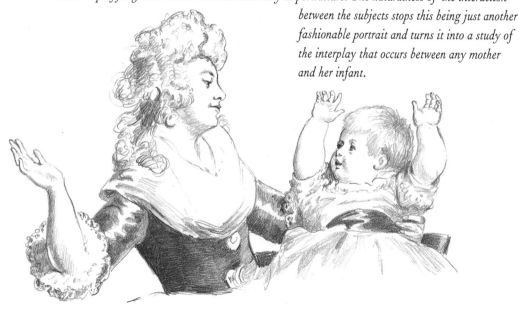

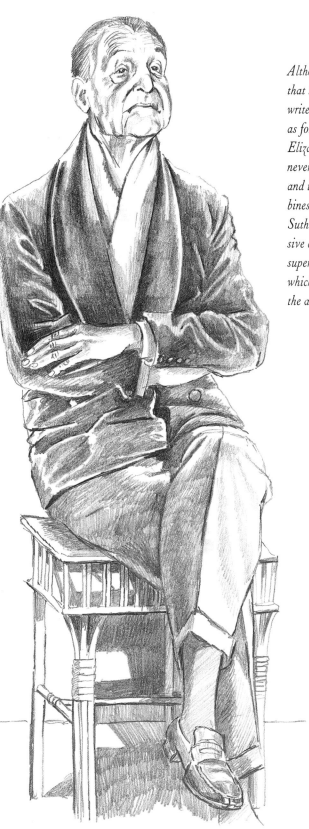

Although the dress and situation suggest that this is an informal portrait, of the writer Somerset Maugham, it is every bit as formal as the pose of Princess Elizabeth opposite. Graham Sutherland never pulled any punches in his portraits and in this example the arm gesture combines with a curiously stiff pose. Sutherland takes advantage of the defensive attitude of the folded arms, the supercilious look and the crossed legs, which don't look any more relaxed than the arms.

Posing: Male Legs

Legs rarely receive the attention accorded the other limbs and only come into their own in a full-length portrait. They can, however, be more than just a pedestal for the rest of the body. In the days when men wore close-fitting nether garments the showing off of the legs was a very masculine statement, often to do with power or wealth. An aristocrat rode a horse and so his legs were often more elegantly proportioned than those of the lowly peasant, whose limbs generally would be shown as more muscular and solid. Many Renaissance paintings use the male form of the legs to tell you something about power, status or wealth, or how fashionable the subjects were as courtiers.

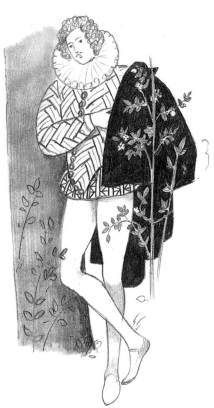

The insouciant pose of this young man leaning against a tree in a rose garden (after Nicholas Hilliard) suggests a moment of romantic, aristocratic idleness. His casually crossed elegant legs stand out against his dark cloak and embroidered doublet. Although we don't know who he is, he has become an icon of the lyrical poetic image of the Elizabethan court.

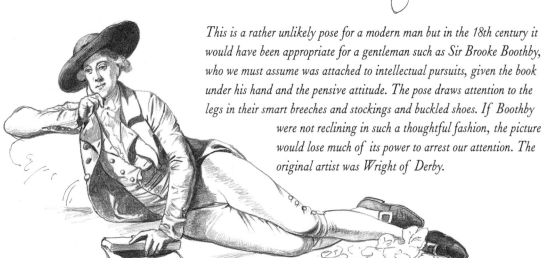

This is a rather unlikely pose for a modern man but in the 18th century it would have been appropriate for a gentleman such as Sir Brooke Boothby, who we must assume was attached to intellectual pursuits, given the book under his hand and the pensive attitude. The pose draws attention to the legs in their smart breeches and stockings and buckled shoes. If Boothby were not reclining in such a thoughtful fashion, the picture would lose much of its power to arrest our attention. The original artist was Wright of Derby.

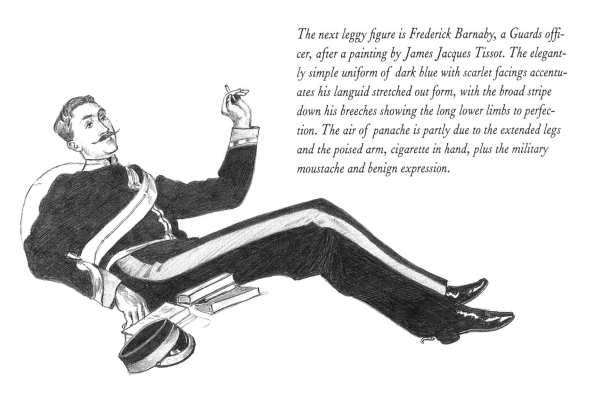

The next leggy figure is Frederick Barnaby, a Guards officer, after a painting by James Jacques Tissot. The elegantly simple uniform of dark blue with scarlet facings accentuates his languid stretched out form, with the broad stripe down his breeches showing the long lower limbs to perfection. The air of panache is partly due to the extended legs and the poised arm, cigarette in hand, plus the military moustache and benign expression.

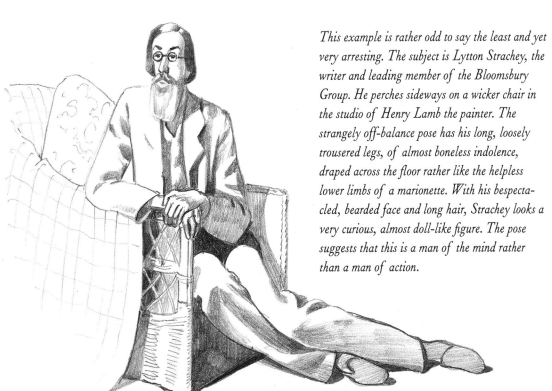

This example is rather odd to say the least and yet very arresting. The subject is Lytton Strachey, the writer and leading member of the Bloomsbury Group. He perches sideways on a wicker chair in the studio of Henry Lamb the painter. The strangely off-balance pose has his long, loosely trousered legs, of almost boneless indolence, draped across the floor rather like the helpless lower limbs of a marionette. With his bespectacled, bearded face and long hair, Strachey looks a very curious, almost doll-like figure. The pose suggests that this is a man of the mind rather than a man of action.

Posing: Female Legs

In our century it is the women who have the upper hand when it comes to making the most of legs; while men have to make do with leg-disguising trousers, women can call on fashion accessories such as high heels and short skirts to show them off. However, until the 20th century, female legs were not much evident in portraits. The first glimpses came in the 19th century, many of them courtesy of Henri de Toulouse-Lautrec, who made a study of the demi-monde and the famous cabaret dancers of his day. The sort of display we see in the first three examples of women's legs on the opposite page was only acceptable at this time if the girls were either actresses or courtesans. Nowadays the revealing of a length of leg by an attractive young woman would be regarded as a modern and wholly appropriate statement. Note the energy and movement in all four examples, and how the legs can be central to the impact of a portrait.

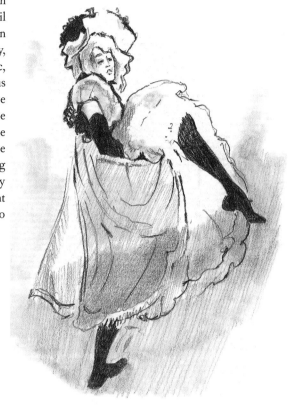

The amazing vigour and liveliness of Jane Avril, a well-loved performer in Lautrec's Paris.

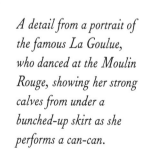

A detail from a portrait of the famous La Goulue, who danced at the Moulin Rouge, showing her strong calves from under a bunched-up skirt as she performs a can-can.

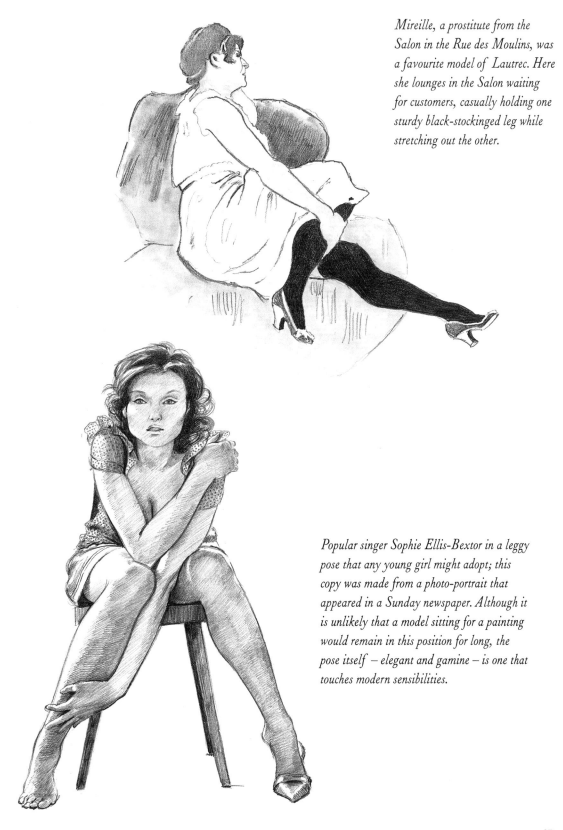

Mireille, a prostitute from the Salon in the Rue des Moulins, was a favourite model of Lautrec. Here she lounges in the Salon waiting for customers, casually holding one sturdy black-stockinged leg while stretching out the other.

Popular singer Sophie Ellis-Bextor in a leggy pose that any young girl might adopt; this copy was made from a photo-portrait that appeared in a Sunday newspaper. Although it is unlikely that a model sitting for a painting would remain in this position for long, the pose itself — elegant and gamine — is one that touches modern sensibilities.

Anatomy of Arms and Legs

The portrait artist doesn't need to go into the anatomy of the hands, arms and legs in any great detail. Usually in a portrait most of the body is covered but sometimes the hands, arms and legs are in evidence, so it is better to have some knowledge of their anatomy, because without this you will not be able to portray them convincingly.

Arm and hand bones

Arm muscles

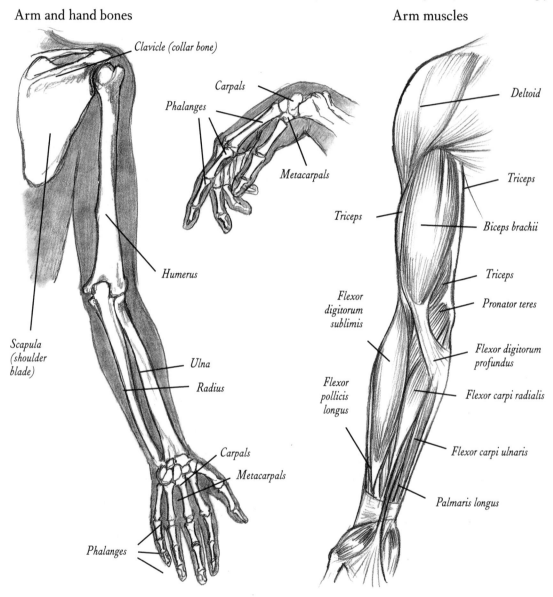

Clavicle (collar bone)

Carpals

Phalanges

Metacarpals

Humerus

Scapula (shoulder blade)

Ulna

Radius

Carpals

Metacarpals

Phalanges

Deltoid

Triceps

Biceps brachii

Triceps

Pronator teres

Triceps

Flexor digitorum sublimis

Flexor digitorum profundus

Flexor pollicis longus

Flexor carpi radialis

Flexor carpi ulnaris

Palmaris longus

Muscle/Function

Triceps: Extension of forearm; adduction of arm
Biceps brachii: Flexion of arm and supination of arm
Pronator teres: Flexion of forearm
Flexor digitorum profundus: Flexion of fingers

Flexor carpi radialis: Flexion and inward rotation of hand
Flexor carpi ulnaris: Flexion of wrist
Palmaris longus: Flexion of hand
Flexor digitorum sublimis: Flexion of middle and distal phalanges of fingers and wrist

Bones of leg

Pelvis

Ilium

Ischium

Pubis

Femur

Patella

Tibia

Fibula

Muscles of leg

Gluteus medius

Iliacus

Psoas major

Pectineus

Adductor brevis

Adductor longis

Gracilis

Sartorius

Rectus femoris

Vastus medialis

Tensor faciae latae

Vastus lateralis

Biceps femoris

Triceps surae

Triceps surae

Peroneus longus

Flexor digitorum longus

Peroneus brevis

Extensor hallucis longus

Bones of foot

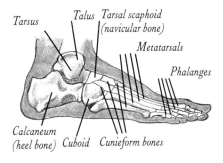

Tarsus

Talus

Tarsal scaphoid (navicular bone)

Metatarsals

Phalanges

Calcaneum (heel bone)

Cuboid

Cunieform bones

Muscle/Function

Gluteus medius: Adduction and medial rotation of thigh

Iliacus: Flexion and medial rotation of femur and flexion of trunk towards thigh

Adductor brevis/longis: Assists in adduction of thigh

Gracilis: Flexion and medial rotation; adduction of thigh

Sartorius: Assists adduction, flexion and lateral rotation of thigh

Rectus femoris: Extension of knee joint

Vastus medialis/lateralis: Flexion and adduction of thigh

Triceps surae: Planar flexion of foot

Flexor digitorus longus: Extension of four lesser toes; assists flexion of foot

Extensor hallucis longus: Extension of great toe

Peroneus brevis: Turns foot sideways

Peroneus longus: Turns and flexes foot; supports arch of foot; steadies leg to assist balance

Biceps femoris: Flexion and medial rotation of leg

Tensor faciae latae: Stretching of fascia tissue; elevation and adduction of thigh

Group and Family Portraits

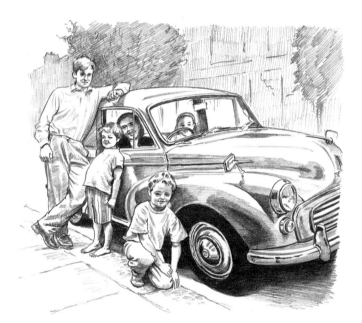

*T*HE ARRANGEMENTS for a group portrait can be almost infinite, because they can be varied depending on how many people you are including. The most obvious grouping is of a family but any number of people who have a professional connection or share some other common ground are candidates for a group portrait. In classical art, for example, there is the famous painting by Rembrandt of the Night Watch. This example also provides an illustration of a problem that can arise with group portraits. Some of the sitters for that famous painting complained that their faces were either too much in shadow or not in prominent enough positions. The overall effect is always more important than the individual likenesses incorporated in a group portrait, but be aware that your drawing is unlikely to please all participants.

However, the greatest problem with a group of people is not being able to get all the people together at the same time. Drawing them separately can make it difficult to relate the different elements together convincingly, but with the right reference and perseverance, it can be done successfully. The reality of modern life means that you must not expect ideal conditions and that you have a sensible contingency plan to cope with absences. The significance of the relationships between the people is as important as the aesthetic nature of the composition. In a family there is always the mater- or paterfamilias to place at the centre. However, in any grouping you will find natural relationships which connect across and within your arrangement and so make the end result more interesting.

There is no one way of grouping just three people, let alone a larger number. Once you begin to consider your grouping, you will find possibilities occurring to you. Take the first interesting arrangement you arrive at and start there. The next time, try something different. Think of this visual world as your plaything, which you can alter according to your wishes and understanding of the moment. As you grow in experience you will undoubtedly experiment more and have a lot of fun in the process.

Setting up Groups

To set up a group portrait you first need to consider how and what is going to be the content. Supposing you know a couple and their son who would like their portrait drawn with all three of them in it. You would need first to consider the individuals you are dealing with. For the sake of the exercise, let's says that the man is thickset and heavy of build, the woman is smaller and matronly, and the boy is slim and small. Consider the following arrangements:

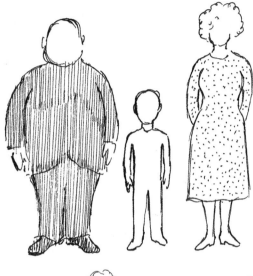

These three subjects constitute the raw material of the picture. There are various ways we might choose to put them together to make a unified composition.

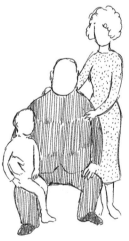

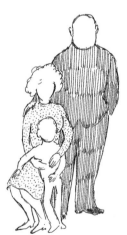

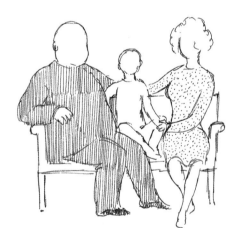

We might place the man on a chair, the boy on his knee and his wife leaning on him, hand on his shoulder.

boy leaning against her legs, and the husband standing with his arm across her shoulders.

with father resting on one arm, mother leaning on the other with her hand across the back of the divan and little boy squatting between them, holding his mother's hand while leaning against his father.

Maybe we sit the lady down, put the

Or we might sit all three on a divan

Taking Your Composition Forward

Once you decide on an arrangement for your figures, you then need to consider their dress (formal or informal); the background (inside or outside, dark or light; detailed or plain); the lighting (from above or the side, strong or diffused); or props (pets, favourite toys, hats, books, musical instruments). And so it goes on; the list is unending. But that is half the fun. From this, you can imagine that you might arrive at an infinite variety of groupings.

Don't exhaust your sitters by trying out too many variations at once. When you've hit on the idea you want to pursue, make a quick sketch of your group in position, without worrying about likeness, and then draw each face in the right position separately, before putting the faces and the group composition together to produce your finished work.

Don't expect your subjects to hold the pose for long periods, especially when children are involved. You won't be in the same position as the great Roman painter of groups of figures, Caravaggio, who, at the height of his fame, paid his models so well that they'd sit, stand and pose for him for days on end.

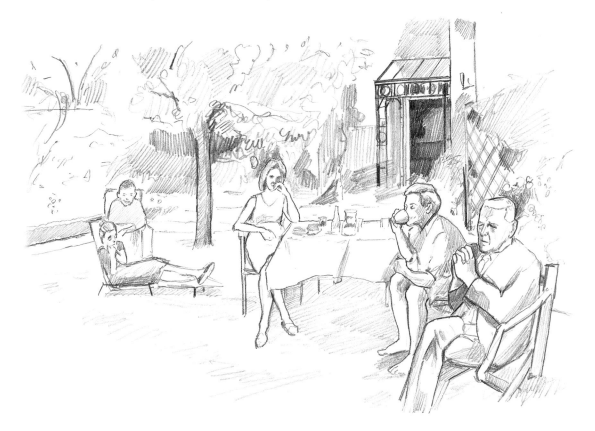

A copy of one of Michael Andrews' first large pieces of work, a group portrait of his family in their garden in Norfolk on a summer afternoon. The original painting is at least six feet high and took two years to complete.

After drawing up a sketch which gave him the positions of the individuals, Andrews then had to make more careful individual studies. He also worked from photographs. The final picture is quite a dynamic composition, spread across the canvas and in some depth from front to back. The drawing of the figures has been kept relatively simple, with the two nearest the viewer the most precisely detailed.

Close Groupings

All sorts of arrangements can make good compositions, and in the process tell us a great deal about the sitters. It used to be the case that a portrait would include clues as to the sitter's position in society or would show to what he (invariably) owed his good fortune. Most artists, however, are more interested in incorporating subtle hints about the nature of the relationships between the subjects in the groups they portray. You may choose to introduce an object into your arrangement as a device to link your subjects.

There are many ways of making a group cohere in the mind and eye of the viewer. In these two examples, both after realist painter Lucian Freud, the closeness of the arrangements is integral to the final result.

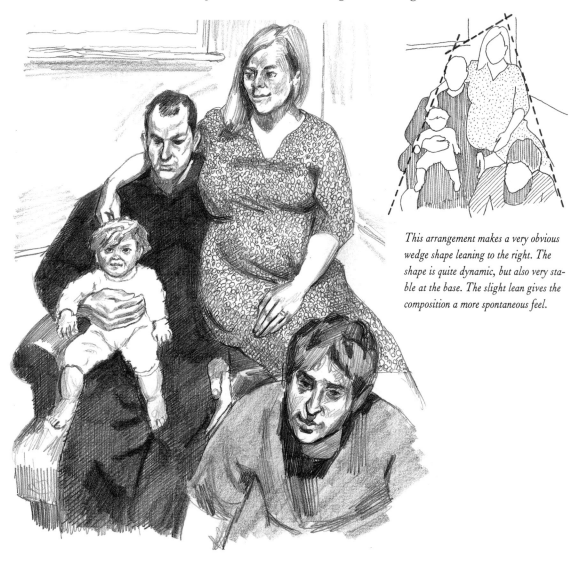

This arrangement makes a very obvious wedge shape leaning to the right. The shape is quite dynamic, but also very stable at the base. The slight lean gives the composition a more spontaneous feel.

The central interest is shared between the baby and his parents. Our eye travels from the infant to the couple as they support him and each other on the armchair. In front, the elder son is slightly detached but still part of the group.

The connection between the parents and the baby is beautifully caught, and the older boy's forward movement, as though he is getting ready to leave the nest, is a perceptive reading of the family dynamic.

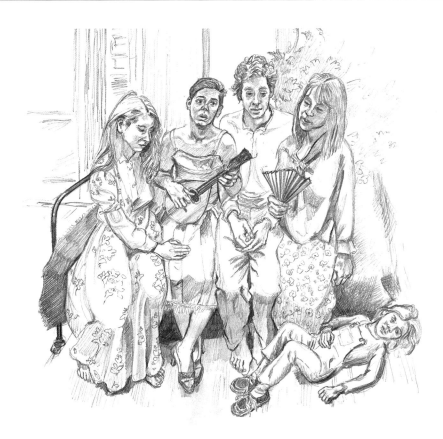

'*Large Interior – after Watteau*' is reminiscent of that artist's *fêtes champêtres* compositions in which young courtiers are depicted listening to music and enjoying each other's company. Freud transmits the outdoors to a well-lit indoor scene with three young women, a young man, and a child lying at their feet. As in many Watteau paintings the girls are wearing rather flowery, pretty dresses and the boy is garbed in a loose white ensemble, rather like a Pierrot. While the whole ensemble makes for a very friendly grouping, there is an element of a more formal mode of arrangement. In Freud's original the space around the figures produces a very posed almost artificial effect. Here, even the child lying at the feet of the quartet seems very conscious of her position in the scene.

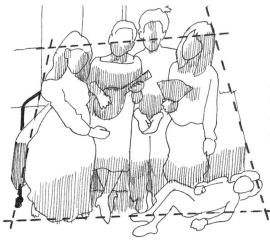

This is a very solid, stable, composed group. The individuals are just lined up along the same base with some squashing together of the upper bodies. The lying down figure is almost like an afterthought and contributes to the portrait's spontaneity.

Centre-Pieces

For a group portrait it can be very effective to include a focal point around which the sitters can gather. In bygone times an unwritten rule of portraiture was that the artist should incorporate devices pin-pointing the social standing and worthiness of the people he painted. Nowadays both artists and sitters are more interested in a presentation that is essentially revealing of character and individuality.

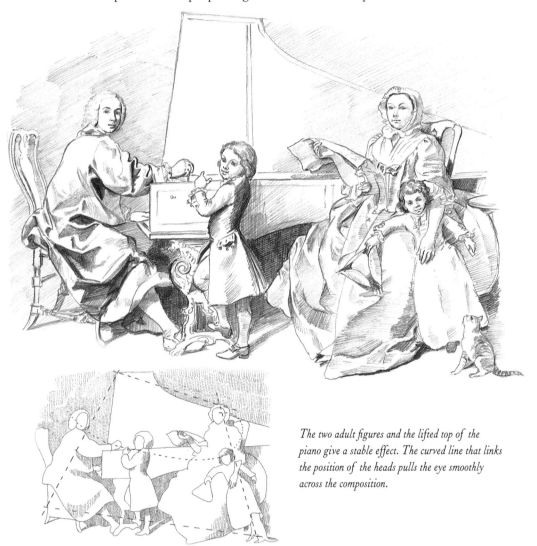

The two adult figures and the lifted top of the piano give a stable effect. The curved line that links the position of the heads pulls the eye smoothly across the composition.

Like many 18th-century portraits this one is carefully posed to include clues to the sitters' social position. The artist, Carl Marcus Tuscher, wants to show us that these people are comfortably off – note the care that has gone into the clothing. The head of the family is Burkat Shudi, a well known harpsichord manufacturer and friend of the composer Handel. The harpsichord is centrally positioned but set behind. If we were not sure that the family owes its good fortune to the instrument, Tuscher underlines the connection by posing Shudi at the keyboard with a tuning fork in his right hand, and has the eldest son indicating to the viewer what his father is doing. The arrangement is balanced but relaxed. It is as though we have dropped in on the family unexpectedly at home and found them at leisure.

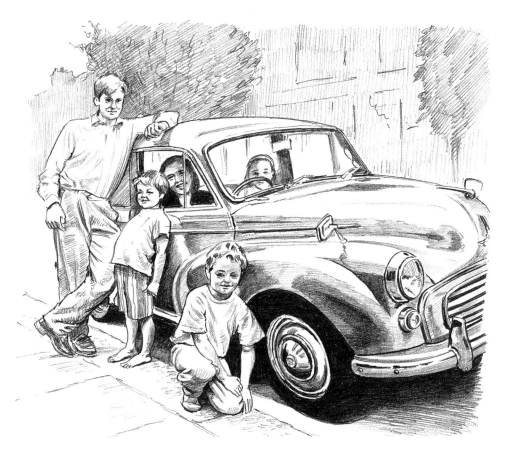

This example might almost be a portrait of the car as much as it is of the family. Obviously very well looked after, polished and shining, it is the centre-piece of the arrangement, if not quite the head of the household. The pride of possession is very evident among the males. The females inside the car are less obvious, although the mother is in the driving seat. This sort of casually posed arrangement is more often found in photo-portraiture. The style makes the drawing of the figures more difficult than it might have been in a different arrangement.

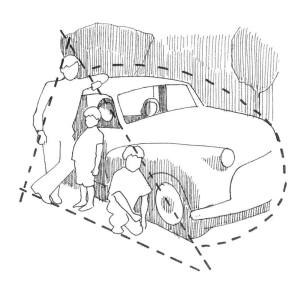

This composition is unusual and rather dynamic, partly due to the position of the car. The three figures outside the car form an acute angled triangle which also gives perspective. The bulge of the car against the longer side of the triangle produces a stabilizing element.

Formal Arrangements

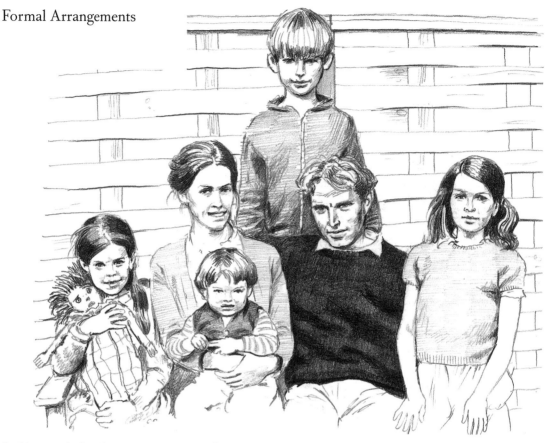

In this example there is an attempt to create a formal pose, but of the kind you get when people have gathered for a snapshot. The father is sitting, as is the mother, who has the youngest child in her lap. The two daughters are perched either side of their parents. The oldest boy only seems to be standing because there is not enough room for him on the same bench, and he is obviously the only one tall enough to look over the top of his father's head.

Another simple enough com-position, with a large triangu-lar shape like a pyramid, with the individual figures radiat-ing outwards from the wide base, like the arms of a fan. Very static and symmetrical.

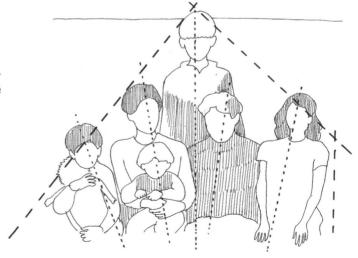

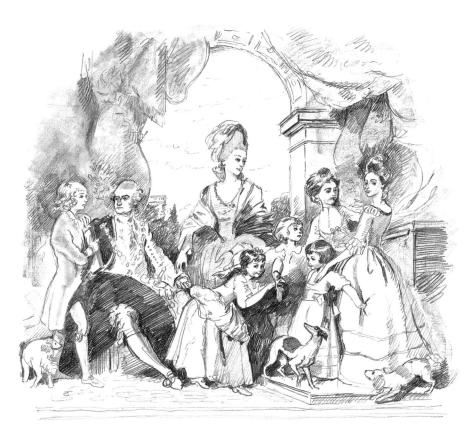

The Duke of Marlborough's family portrait was done by Sir Joshua Reynolds in his best classical manner. We see the father seated in the grandeur of the robes of the Order of the Garter, his hand resting on the shoulder of his eldest son. The mother stands at the back of the group under the triumphal arch, her fingers gently resting on her husband's cuff as she casts an amused glance at her children. They are grouped along the space in front of her, dogs weaving around their feet. One young girl is holding a mask, trying to frighten her sister, who is leaning back against an older girl's dress. Reynolds has lightened the formality with this humorous touch to bring out the characters of his sitters. This may be a great family, but there is a human dimension.

The drawing style for this copy is loose and tonally sparse. Areas of tone are either heavily scribbled lines, meandering lines following the form or smudged pencil to make the texture as unobtrusive as possible. The outlines are correct but not detailed. Simplification is a good rule here.

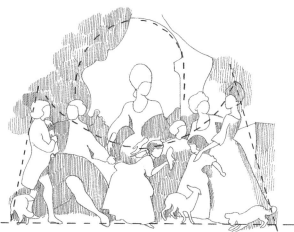

Note the nicely balanced wedge shape with the wide curve of the heads of the family. The exception is the Duchess who is centred under the tall arch in the background. Mobile, but restful at the same time.

99

Breaking with Convention

Most of the arrangements we have looked at so far have been formal in terms of their composition and very obviously posed. The approach taken in this next drawing is remarkable. The English painter, William Hogarth, was notable for his progressive social attitudes, and these are very much to the fore in this powerful and humane piece of work, in which he presents his servants.

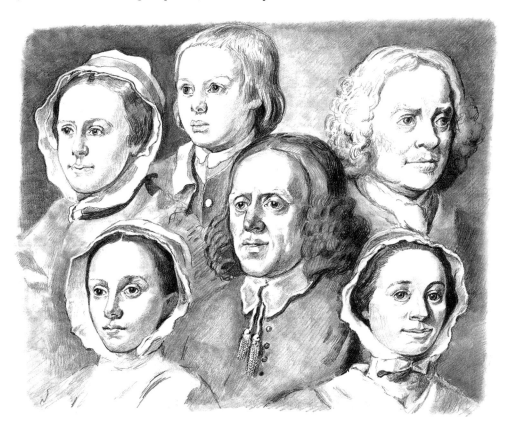

The original Hogarth painting from which this copy was made is an extraordinary essay in characterization. Executed with great brilliance and obvious warmth and sincerity, it shows the artist's servants. The composition is exemplary. Each head, although obviously drawn separately, has been placed in a balanced design in which each face has its own emphasis. Hogarth's interest in his subjects is evident from the lively expressions, and we feel we are getting genuine insights from a man who knew these people well.

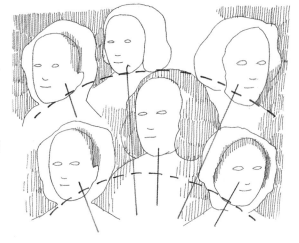

A very straightforward fanning out of the six heads from the base, placed in close proximity. All slightly off-centre but still very symmetrical.

Double Portraits

The double portrait can be used to produce very interesting effects of juxtaposition, by placing two similar, or two very dissimilar, people alongside each other in order to create contrast or repetition. There are some very famous examples of this approach, but in the next series I have chosen particular illustrations that ring the changes visually and show how easily the device can be used to produce an unusual picture.

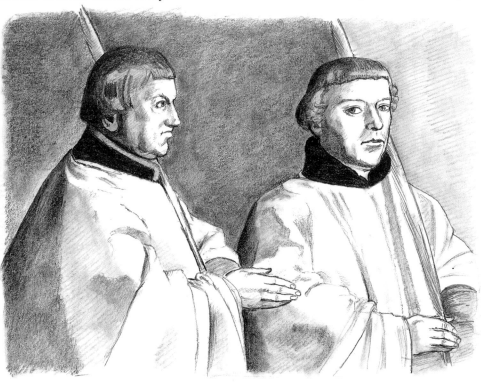

This rather stylized portrait of two canons, connected in religious orders and devotional intent, is made powerful by the simple repetition of shape and size. In Tudor times clerics were the most respected of the non-aristocratic community, and considerable attention was paid to their image for the public. These two are shown as formal and detached from the viewer, but nevertheless wanting to show their status in the community. At this time the full-length portrait was reserved for rulers. Bust portraits such *as this, like Roman classical busts, were a way of men from good families showing that they were solid citizens and of good intent. The inference is: 'We are not saints, but pious believers'.*

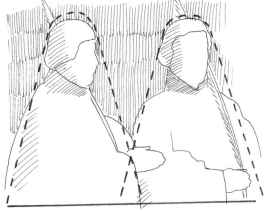

Very stable, very straightforward arrangement like two truncated triangles.

Obvious Doubles

Usually an artist does not get round to drawing a double unless someone specifically asks for it. Very often parents with two children will choose to have their offspring painted or drawn in this way, and it is a favourite method of married couples celebrating important anniversaries.

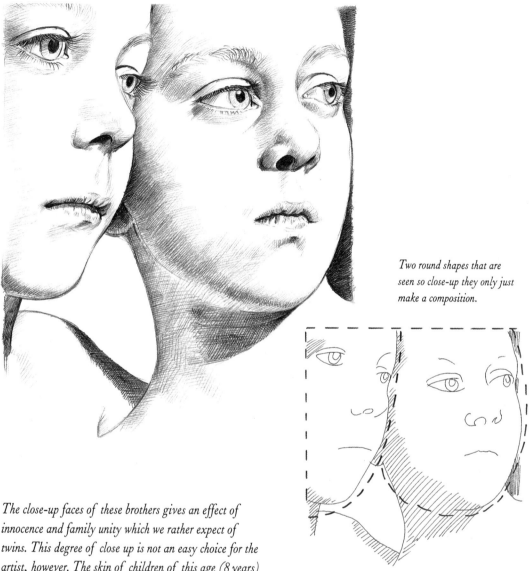

Two round shapes that are seen so close-up they only just make a composition.

The close-up faces of these brothers gives an effect of innocence and family unity which we rather expect of twins. This degree of close up is not an easy choice for the artist, however. The skin of children of this age (8 years) is always so smooth and the bone structure largely hidden by the rounded flesh that there are no lines of stress or tension to help give an accurate rendering. In such circumstances you have to measure out the face – and quickly, because the average 8-year-old will not sit still for very long, and their faces are also very mobile.

This drawing was made from an excellent photograph by Jane Chilvers which won a photographic portrait award and now hangs in the National Portrait Gallery in London. The original was a very detailed and rather cool image. I didn't attempt to put in too much surface detail because, to my eye, the smoothness of the facial surface is part of the charm.

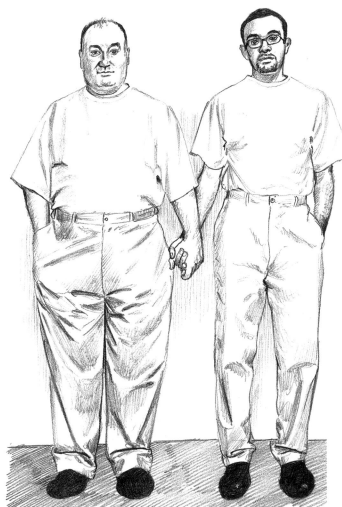

The pose in this father-and-son portrait – taken from a photograph by John Nassari – suggests a sense of humour in the artist and a sort of family complicity about the portrait. However, despite the humour, the effect is fairly cool and detached. The uniform clothing gives the pair an oddly dressed up quality although what they are wearing is very ordinary. The drawing is simple and mainly concerned with the outline. It demonstrates that if you get the main shape right, individual qualities can shine through.

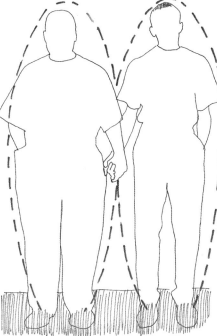

The two vertical ellipses overlapping in the centre make this a stable and uncomplicated arrangement.

Couples

The reason behind the vast majority of double portraits is that there is a personal or professional connection between the two sitters. Unsurprisingly, most double portraits are of husbands and wives. We show two historical examples followed by two contemporary views.

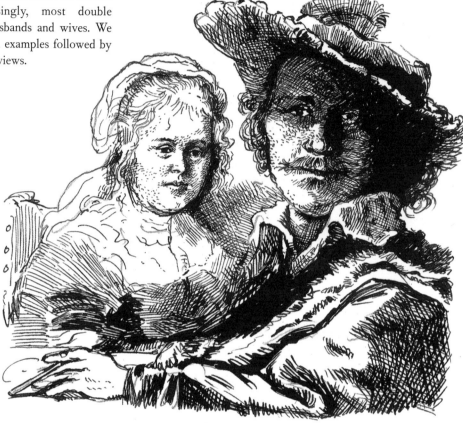

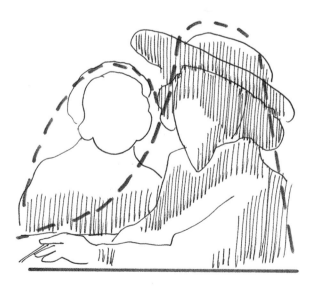

This double portrait of Rembrandt and his wife looks a bit odd because she is set back behind her husband. Possibly the artist had to use a mirror to assist in drawing them both and as a result she would necessarily be a bit behind him in perspective. He has tried to balance the effect by showing his own face in shadow and highlighting that of his wife.

The composition is not very obvious. The front shape of the head and arm of Rembrandt acts like a holding shape for the smaller shape of his wife, who gives the appearance of a ventriloquist's doll.

In Gainsborough's marvellous portrait of the
Duke and Duchess of Cumberland the
arrangement does not attempt to disguise the fact
that the young wife is much taller than her
princely military husband. The full-length figures
stop the picture being intimate. There is a definite
'swagger' effect, as the pair seem to be stepping
out in public to show themselves off.

   This sort of drawing needs a feathery, rather
impressionistic touch with the pencil, using loose
lines but observing the shapes as accurately as
possible so that the lines don't become too
arbitrary. A considered effort to draw in the soft,
feathery lines works better than making swift,
dashing strokes.

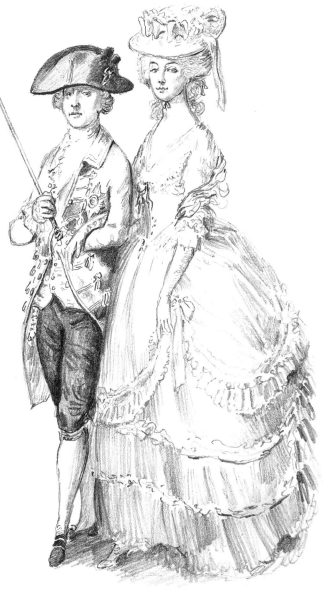

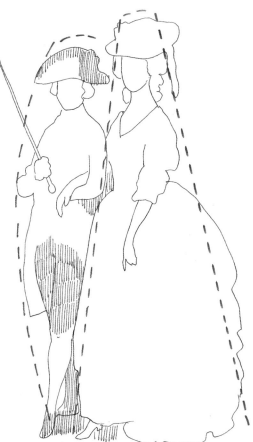

*The tall elongated triangle of the Duchess
makes a strong, vertical base shape for the
rounder ellipse of her husband.*

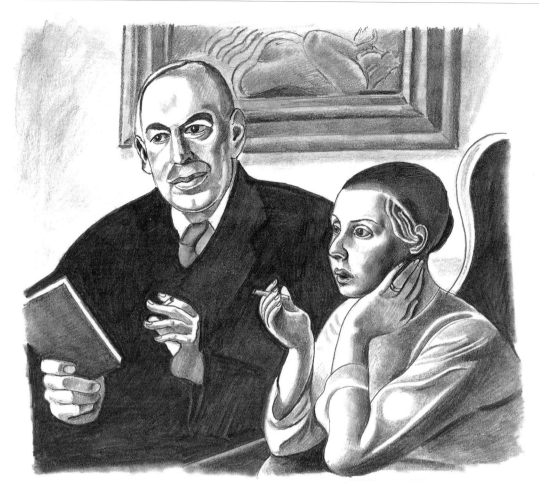

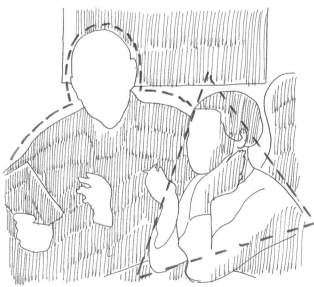

The economist John Maynard Keynes commissioned a double portrait of himself and his wife from painter William Roberts. The rather simple Cubist style was Roberts' normal way of working, although usually you could not recognize a human form in his paintings. The slightly mechanistic look of reducing all the shapes to cylinders and ovoid forms tends to give a statuesque but rather inhuman look to his sitters, who could almost be dolls. Even so there is enough individuality in the two figures in this portrait to give an interesting, if unintentionally humorous, effect.

The large amorphous shape of Keynes acts as a comfortable foil to the sharp equilateral triangle shape of his wife.

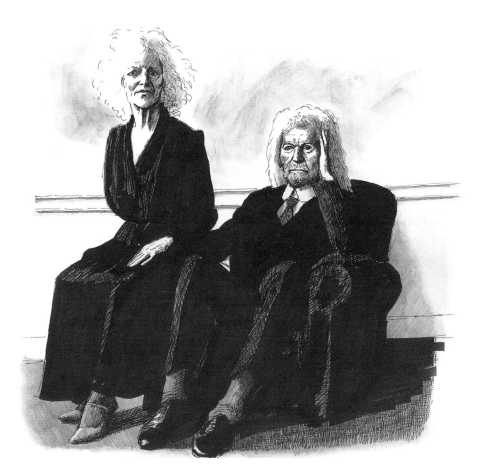

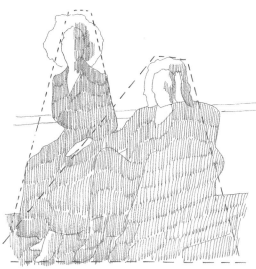

The large dark triangular shape of the man makes a strong definite statement with the tall narrow cone of his wife growing out of the same base.

This drawing of an elderly couple posed together (originally for a photograph) is an interesting mix of formal and informal. The composition of the two figures is neat and the arrangement rather unusual. The dark suit, stiff collar and tie of the man and the dark, severe dress of the woman is softened by long and brushed out white hair. The man's straggly beard and the way he is leaning on his hand, and she is perched on the arm of his chair, lend a naturalness to the drawing and give some indication of character and a way of life.

The outline drawing was done in pencil and then gone over in ink. The dark areas were blocked in and didn't require any texture. The faces, hair and hands needed a softer touch.

Life through the Ages

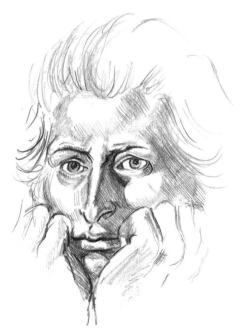

WE HAVE ALREADY LOOKED at the problems of composing portraits, as well as devising settings and backgrounds for them. Later we shall be considering the personal accoutrements that can be used to convey character and mood. However, the essence of any portrait, and what tells us most about any individual, is how they look. How people look is determined by many factors, not least their age. Portrait artists are obsessed with conveying what they see and feel when presented with a subject. Their view comes out in the way they handle the texture and quality of the skin, eyes and hair and the myriad subtle touches they incorporate to show age and condition. This approach is especially true of the masters of drawing, whose work reveals lessons that we latter-day students of art, who are so affected by our reading of photographic evidence of age, would do well to learn.

We have been so influenced by our exposure to film, television, video and photography that when we look at a visual scene we see it as though it has been refined through the lens of a master cameraman. We are used to multiple images, and can quickly cross-cut between them without difficulty. Our eyes and mind, like that of a camera, zoom in on details, isolating actions and giving us a much less unifed view of what we see.

When we draw, there is a danger of looking for specific points of interest to the detriment of the whole picture. In the context of portraits this often means that we read the graphic possibilities of an expression rather than seeing the underlying anatomy. We may end up with an expressive portrait but not a structurally truthful one. We may actually believe a person looks like our drawing of them until we catch them in an unusual light or situation and suddenly are presented with new depths. The relatively superficial knowledge of the human face exposed by photography is no substitute for knowledge of anatomy, which gives a solid structural basis for all types of portraiture.

Portraying Different Ages

As a portrait artist you have to assess correctly the age of the face in front of you so that it can be shown without causing the sitter to feel that you have made them look older or younger. Making people look younger is not normally a problem because most of us have an image of ourselves as younger than we are in reality.

The hardest individuals to draw, oddly enough, are the very young. First and foremost, they can't pose for you. Secondly, baby faces have very little in the way of distinctive features and therefore are very difficult to make interesting. As I hope you will see from the following series of drawings, the older we become the richer are the opportunities for the artist.

(Unless stated otherwise, a B grade pencil was used for all the pencil drawings in this series.)

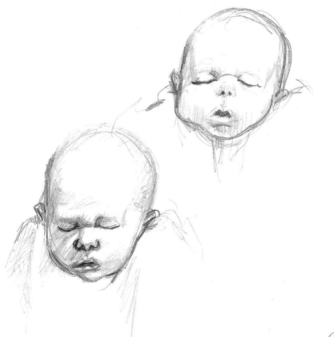

4 weeks: Drawing a young baby is a very salutary exercise, because the features at this age are not distinctive enough to allow a satisfactory result. Indeed the baby's mother is very likely the only person to whom the features are significantly different from those of any other baby of the same age. The most sensible way of tackling a portrait of this sort is to wait until the baby is fast asleep and then concentrate on placing the eyes, nose, mouth and ears accurately relative to the whole head. Apart from making sure that the head is also drawn accurately, this really is the best you can do in the circumstances.

6 months: At this age the face is becoming a bit more distinctive, because of a widening repertoire of expressions and the addition of hair. Pen and ink is not ideal for drawing a child this young, but as this was a spontaneous portrait I used what was to hand.

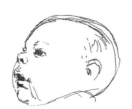
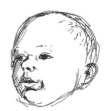

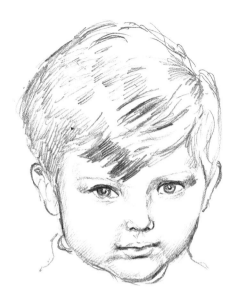

3 years: It is not easy to get young children to sit still for long, which is why drawings of them are often small. Luckily this chap managed not to wriggle for about five minutes at a time, giving me just long enough to capture his clear, bright, lively expression. His eyes and mouth moved a lot, so I also took a photograph to help me in the finished pencil drawing. The technique is careful and as exact as possible. The expression is easy enough if you get the proportions of eyes, nose and mouth correct within the shape of the head. Note the large area of the top of the head; the proportion at this age is unlike that of the adult head, the chin being much smaller in proportion to the rest of the skull.

4 years: Two tones of conté pencil were put in carefully with as light a touch as possible to produce this example on toned paper. The hair is smooth and relatively easy to draw. The main interest is in the face, with the eyes particularly arresting, and the soft blurred look of the snub nose and soft mouth. The tone over the side of the face and around the nose and mouth had to be put in fairly lightly to prevent the surface looking harsh or angular. The absence of sharp edges in the features meant that the pencil had to be gently stroked onto the paper.

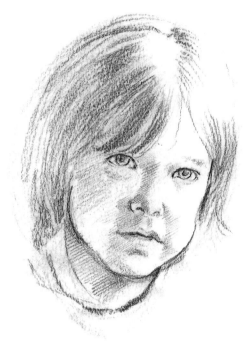

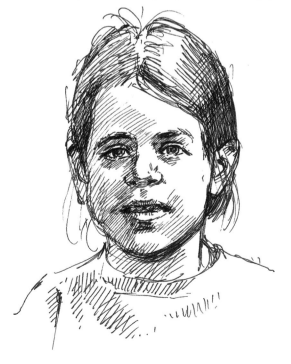

5 years: Ink is a difficult medium for a face as unformed as this and so the style had to be fairly loose and fluid. I used sweeping lines to prevent them looking too dry and technical. Ink does not allow a lot of subtle variations but its very simplicity can give a drawing great strength.

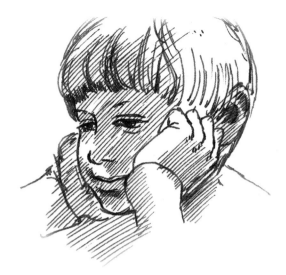

6 years: In this small sketch with a ball-point pen I was interested in capturing the shape of the head and the dimensional effect of the large area of shadow and the bright areas catching the light. The features are drawn simply in line to show through the overall texture of shadow. At this age the features are becoming better defined, allowing the use of a stronger line.

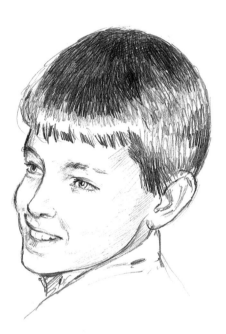

10 years: Although the face is still very young at this age the lines can be drawn more crisply and definitely. The shiny, short hair produces a nice contrast with the face. The features are clearly drawn but with little tone to capture the fresh, clear look which is typical of children of this age.

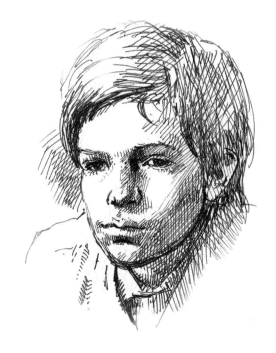

13 years: In this example in ink the toned paper gives a slightly heavy look to the face which, although still soft and relatively unmarked by experience, has a slightly stronger bone structure and a dour uncertain look expressive of the mood swings that beset youngsters around this age.

15 years: The face has the clarity and charm of youth but in the expression there is a hint of deeper knowledge. Drawing a portrait of this age group is not easy for the artist and is largely a question of what you leave out rather than what you put in. Often you can end up making your subject look older than young adults who are several years their senior. The beauty of the form demands clarity in the drawing. Further than this you have to try to express in some way the expectant feelings that girls of this age experience.

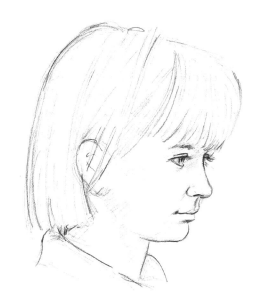

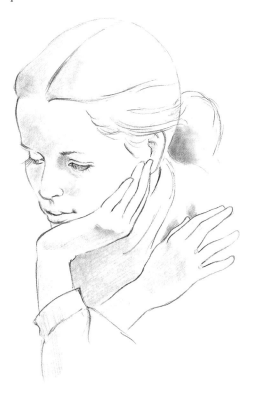

16 years: At this age the features are complete in form and full of life, strongly marked but still fresh and untouched by real anxieties. A light touch is required. Here the features are clearly drawn and there was an opportunity for making much of the hairstyle.

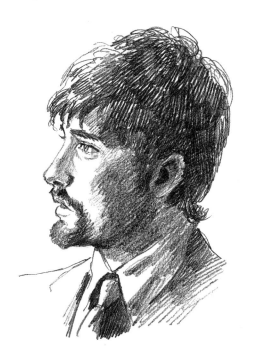

20 years: There is plenty of form to draw at this age and the greater maturity in style and carriage provides opportunities for interest. The beard growth and sculpted bones showing through help to define the age nicely. A 2B grade pencil was used in addition to a B grade.

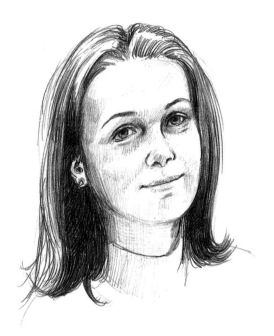

25 years: The personality is now very definite and tends to come through in any drawing in any style. As before the features and head shape have to be kept clear and definite, but you will have to pay careful attention to detail to convey distinctive nuances of expression and attitude.

33 years: In the thirties, experience of the world begins to tell on the face. The artist needs to identify the main characteristic of the subject and then bring into it all the subtle psychological variations that are shown in expression, habitual lines on the face and ambiguity in the projection of personality.

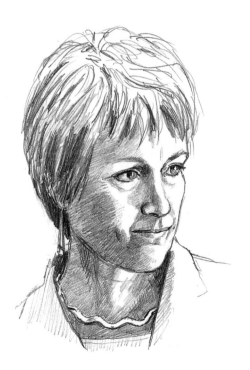

50 years: At the half century mark the artist is presented with a range of experience to emphasize or play down. You can opt for craggy weathered surfaces, volatile expressions of emotion, the more benign influences registered on the face or a more generalized form that reduces the wear and tear to a texture of soft marks. Whatever you decide, it will not be difficult to see how to put down the structure. At this age there is plenty to draw. The media used were B and 2B grade pencils.

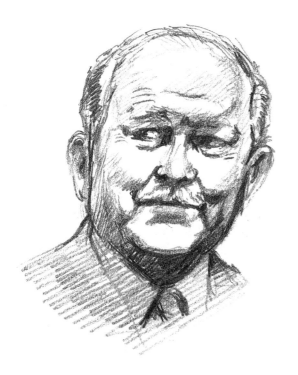

70 years: The features show very definite marks by this age. Lines are firmly engraved on the face and dilapidation of the surface textures and hair is very evident. However, if the person's experience has been in the main of a pleasant nature the face will have wisdom, benignity and, often, good humour. All is revealed and is not difficult to draw.

80 years: This particular subject is very well preserved and sprightly, but with all the lines and wrinkles associated with old age. Her expression shows what she is like; it is almost as impossible to dissimulate at this age as it is at the very youngest. The artist is presented with a map of a whole career, which can be fascinating to draw. Careful drawing is required to get across the texture of the features and the expression. The media used were B and 2B grade pencils and a stub.

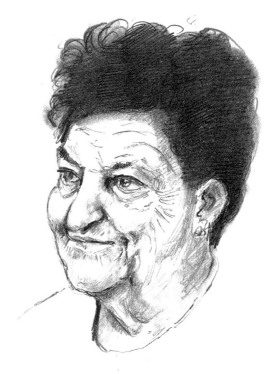

Master Strokes

In the following pages we look at some examples of the changing ages of humanity as seen through the eyes of some of the great artists. In earlier periods it may have been true that people aged more quickly because life was physically much harder, and so someone depicted in their middle years will look far older than would their equivalent in age now. However, if you study these remarkable portraits purely from the standpoint of the way the subtle signs of youth or age are shown on the human face,

you will find them immensely instructive. Some will look almost elementary in their simplicity. Closer examination will reveal the tremendous skill it takes to reduce complex subtle effects to such a degree.

Every mark you make on a drawing gives some information, even if it is just that you are unsure of what you've seen. In every portrait you attempt your observation is paramount. Never forget this: the best results always derive from observation and attention to detail, as the work of the great artists proves.

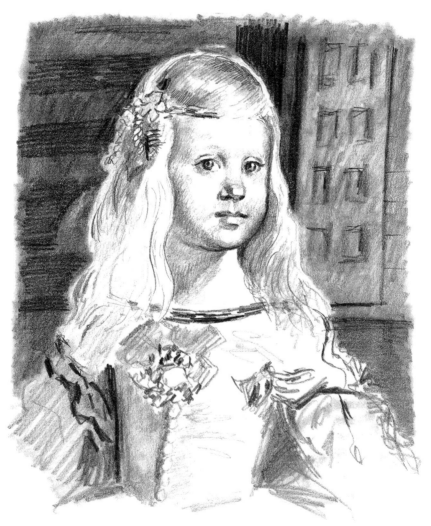

Velázquez's portrait of the five-year-old Infanta of Spain captures the innocence of early childhood. The sweetness of her expression contrasts with the dark background and her stiff formal dress, accentuating her innocence. Soft black pencil (B) and graphite stick (2B) were used for this copy. With the exception of the edges of the eyes and the dress, the lines were kept sparse and light. The broad edge of the graphite produced the dusky background tones.

The original of this portrait of a dreamy ten-year-old boy, by Antonella da Messina, was done in silverpoint. A B pencil was used throughout, producing closely grouped lines with a little cross-hatching on the face and very sharp, clear lines around the eyes, mouth and for the main strands of hair.

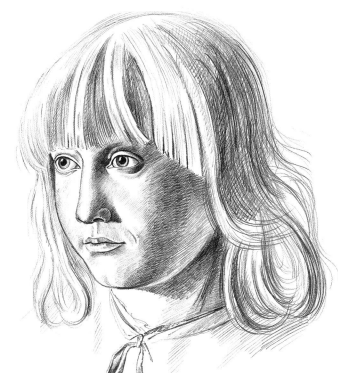

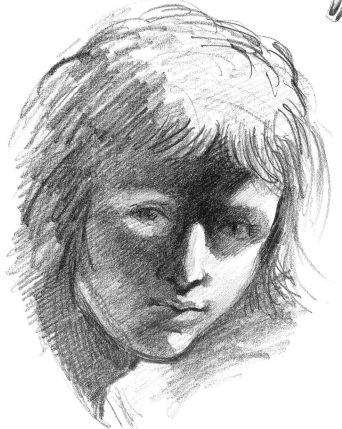

Guercino (Giovanni Barbieri) conveys the idea of youth moving towards womanhood in his original drawing of a fifteen-year-old girl. To capture the sfumato effect, a 2B was mainly used to produce the smudgy dark areas, supported by a 4B. The technique was fairly even strokes in the same direction, except for the hair.

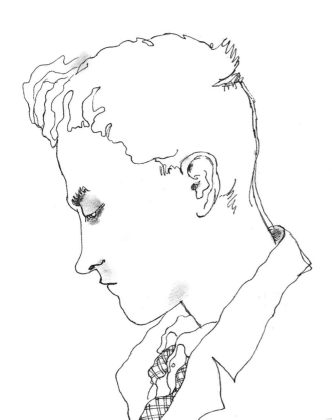

Jean Cocteau's brilliant line drawing of Jean Desbordes, who was about seventeen at the time, captures the softness of youth together with a certain gangly self-consciousness in the downcast head and glance. The slightly wayward hair and loosely tied necktie adds to the air of youthful carelessness. The key to the drawing is the absence of tone and the thin, continuous wavy lines. My copy was drawn with a .01 Japanese pigment ink pen.

This copy of a portrait of Gabrielle d'Estrees by a follower of François Clouet was executed by carefully stroking on lines of soft B and 2B pencil. In some areas chalk was carefully put in. Sharp lines have been applied only around the eyes, nostrils and mouth. Clouet reveals her as wary and self-composed beyond her eighteen years, and yet we are not convinced this is more than a pose.

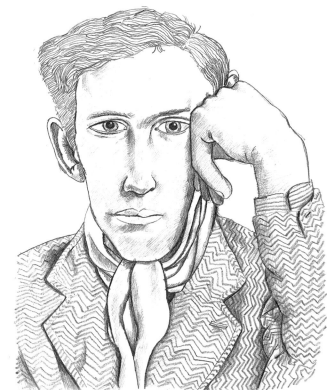

Lucien Freud's drawing of a
young man in his early twenties
emphasizes large hands and long
features, giving an angular awkwardness to an otherwise composed and calm portrait.
In this copy the pencil lines are
incisive with minimal shading.
The herringbone pattern on the
jacket was done with a blunter
point to achieve softer lines.

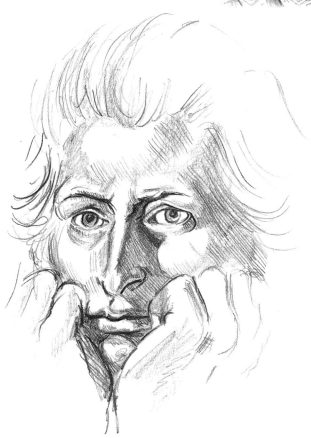

Henry Fuseli drew this self-portrait when he was in his thirties.
It shows the anxieties and self-
doubt of someone mature enough
to be aware of his own shortcom-
ings. B and 2B soft pencils were
used for this copy to capture the
dark and light shadows as well as
the sharply defined lines depicting
the eyes, nose and mouth.

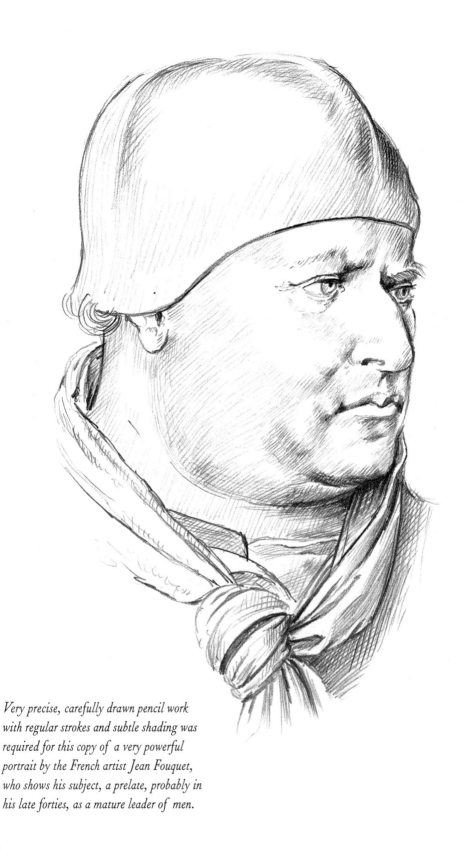

*Very precise, carefully drawn pencil work
with regular strokes and subtle shading was
required for this copy of a very powerful
portrait by the French artist Jean Fouquet,
who shows his subject, a prelate, probably in
his late forties, as a mature leader of men.*

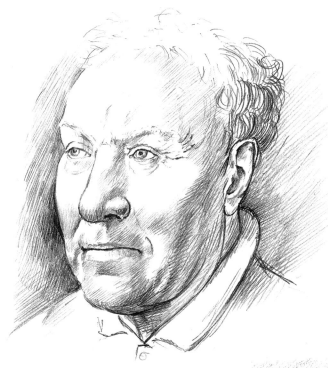

We happen to know that the sitter of this portrait by Jan Van Eyck, the Cardinal of Sante Croce, Florence, is fifty-six years old. The lines of the eyes, ears, nose, mouth and outline of the face are precise and give clear signs of the ageing process. The technique is generally smooth and light with some cross-hatching in the tonal areas. Although Van Eyck portrays his subject as still powerful, there is also a sense of resignation.

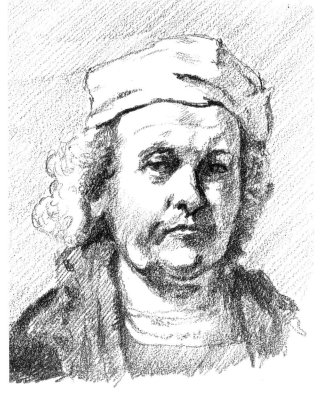

Rembrandt drew himself throughout his life, from early adulthood until just before his death, and has left us an amazing record of his ageing countenance. In this copy of a self-portrait done when he was about sixty years old, a smudgy technique with a soft 2B pencil was used in imitation of the chalk in the original.

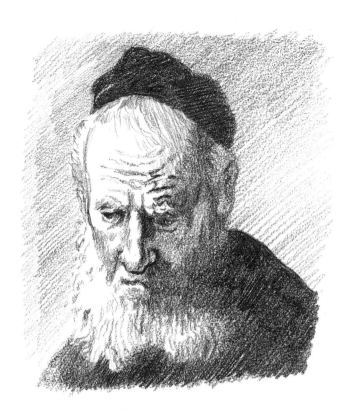

The definition in this copy of Rembrandt's portrait of his father, who was in his early seventies, derives from the use of tonal areas instead of lines. The technique with the pencil is very smudgy and creates an effect that is very similar to one you would get with chalk.

Drawn in pen and ink, after Guercino, these two examples are graphic depictions of the ravages of age, although there is no record of how old the men were. I tried to emulate Guercino's methods, using bold strokes in some places (hair and hood) with tentative broken lines.

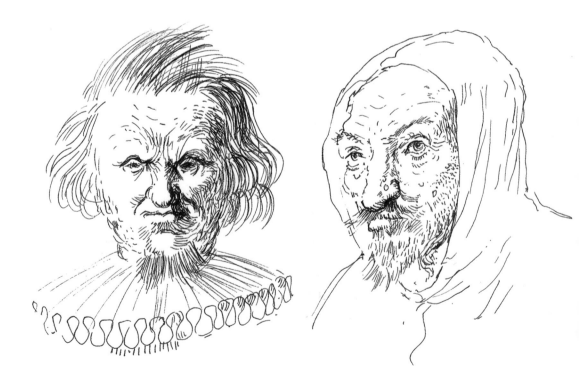

A copy in chalk of a portrait of Jean Edouard Vuillard's mother,
done when she was in her eighties, describes age in a most economic
way. Echoing the original, I was sparing with the tone and detail,
and allowed the wavering lines to follow the gentle disintegration
of the flesh on the face.

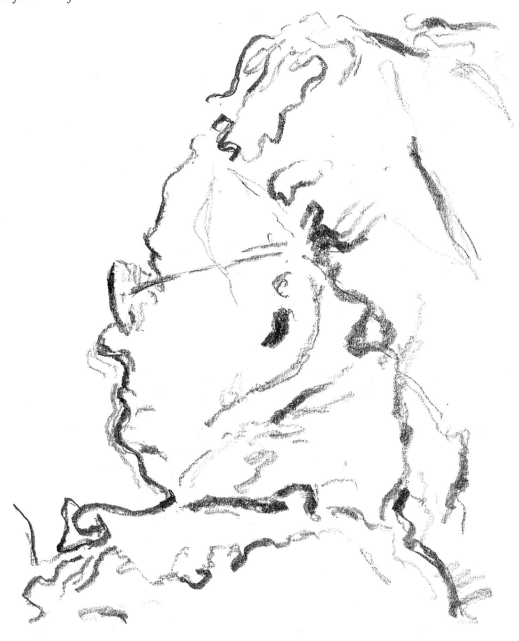

Dress

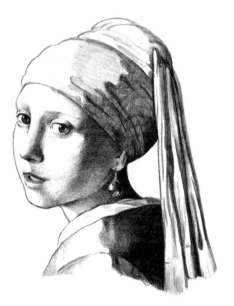

*T*RADITIONALLY PORTRAITS have been used to set a figure within his or her context in society, and there is no easier or more obvious way of doing this than through clothes or accessories.

Historically many portraits tell us quite a lot about the fashions and styles of different periods, but not always quite what you might call 'street fashion'. Dress can give us a clear idea of a sitter's position in the community, and in most portraits – even today – makes a significant contribution to the image being projected. In the past members of royalty were painted in their royal robes and sometimes even wearing a crown. Leaders of the military were shown in their uniforms with insignia to distinguish them from the ordinary warrior. Aristocrats were portrayed adorned with orders and decorations. Academics were often posed in their academic gowns, as were doctors of the church and prelates. Women, of course, were usually shown covered in jewellery of symbolic relevance or as reflections of status.

On occasion you will find that sitters demand that you show a specific item in your portrait of them, or those commissioning you may expect the subject to be portrayed in a certain way. Once I had to paint a small head and neck portrait of a young lady who was most insistent that I show very clearly the pearl earrings she was wearing. These had been a gift from her fiancé, and without their inclusion the portrait would have had no meaning for her. A young boy who hero-worships David Beckham might want to be shown in the Manchester United strip, right down to the appropriate logos. You might have a subject who enjoys fancy dress and losing themselves in another persona.

Personal touches can provide unexpected opportunities for the artist to make a portrait interesting. Long dresses, robes of all kinds, including bathrobes and dressing gowns, can make interesting folds which contribute to the aesthetic quality of a drawing. Necklaces, bracelets, hair clips, ribbons, hats and other accessories also offer opportunities for adding something special. A great deal of fun can be had with dress, so don't overlook the possibilities it provides for adding a dash of sartorial splendour to your portraits.

Matching Dress and Pose

To achieve a good final result, you have to ensure that your sitter accepts the decisions you make about your portrayal of them. If you get them to work with you in deciding the style of dress and the pose you will find the process much easier. Deciding what will work best in a given situation can be great fun and, for the sitter, take some of the tedium out of holding a pose.

A helpful practice in portraiture is to think of some friends or acquaintances and, given what you know about their character and interests, pose and dress them in a way that will communicate some knowledge of them to a disinterested viewer. Enlarge on their own ideas of themselves by suggesting a colour or type of dress. Below are a few examples for you to consider.

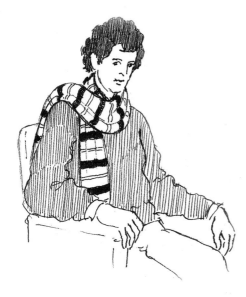

The romantic type, perhaps with literary or thespian interests — something of this quality would be conveyed by posing him with a scarf thrown carelessly around his neck and shoulders.

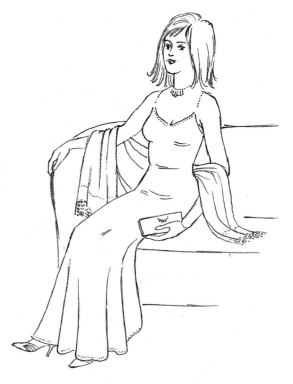

A young girl celebrating a birthday or similar occasion — you could perhaps persuade her to pose in a long dress with shawl, fashion purse and jewellery and try to get across youthful confidence and charm.

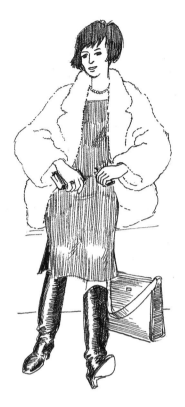

The supermum who manages to hold down a professional job as well as bring up her kids and be a wonderful hostess – she would have to be shown as someone who has multiple calls on her time. Here she is portrayed as well dressed, energetic, obviously just about to go off somewhere – perhaps to a meeting or to collect the kids. The smart bag, cellphone and personal organizer are signs of her hectic life.

A youngster with a sporting passion – he could be shown with the gear which typifies his enthusiasm, in this instance a suitably sun-'n-sand T-shirt and a surfboard, lovingly and proudly displayed.

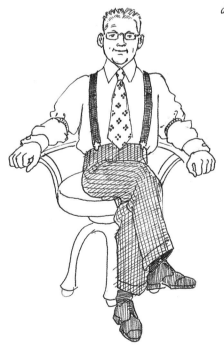

And we all know at least one master-of-the-universe tycoon-to-be who could be seen in power braces and sharp suit, looking confidant as though he's just beaten the market for the umpteenth time.

Dressing for the Part

Getting a subject to wear something out of the ordinary can bring a refreshingly different dimension to a portrait. In the following series of drawings each subject is dressed up to make a statement and the artist has made the most of the drama or beauty of the dress chosen.

In the first three examples we see the sort of dress that might be worn because of the subject's position. Most societies have some sort of hierarchy in dress, a code that helps to define the individual's role and is clearly understood by others. This is almost like a uniform but not totally so.

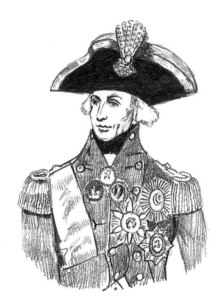

In this copy of an official portrait by William Beechey, Lord Nelson is depicted wearing the dress of an admiral of the Royal Navy. The panache in his cocked hat was a gift of the Sultan of Turkey in recognition of his naval victories, and most of the 'gongs' he wears were awarded to him by foreign royalty. Nelson is shown wearing these honours above those given him by the British and is perhaps making the point that the English monarch was rather slow to give him the top honours to which he felt he was entitled.

Shah Jihan, the Mogul Emperor of India in the 17th century, is presented as an icon of piety and civilised power. The official miniature portrait shows an aureole around his feathered turban, a beautiful silk robe or caftan, jewelled sword and colourful trousers and slippers.

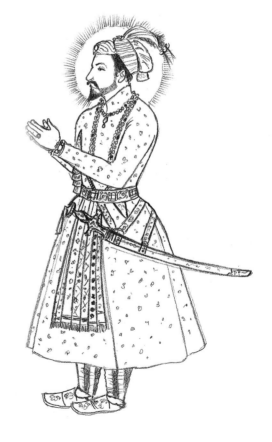

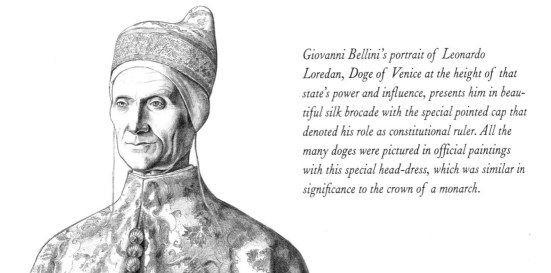

Giovanni Bellini's portrait of Leonardo
Loredan, Doge of Venice at the height of that
state's power and influence, presents him in beautiful silk brocade with the special pointed cap that
denoted his role as constitutional ruler. All the
many doges were pictured in official paintings
with this special head-dress, which was similar in
significance to the crown of a monarch.

Lord Byron in Albanian costume, by Thomas Phillips.
By the time of this portrait (1813), Lord Byron was
famous for his best-selling poetry, his love life and his lib-
eral views. His portrayal in the costume of an Albanian
chieftain is an advertisement of his role as freedom fighter
and a statement on his sympathy with nationalistic causes
in the Hellenic world, where the Albanians and Greeks
fought to free their countries from Turkish rule.

Dressing for Impact

There is always the desire for sitters to look their best for a portrait. Throughout history people have done this, usually to underline their wealth, taste or social position. But as we have already seen, with the portrait of Byron, dressing up to play a role can be immensely rewarding. The artist certainly gets more out of the unusual than the familiar, and for the viewer drama and a sense of occasion are more satisfying than the mundane.

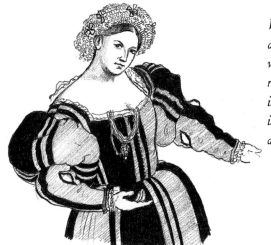

We see here Lucrezia Borgia in an extraordinary dress with an unusual wreath around the head which has the appearance of corkscrew curls of raffia with silk bows on it. In the original painting, by Venetian artist Lorenzo Lotto, the dress is in red and black velvet. The entire ensemble and the pose make this a real 'swagger' portrait.

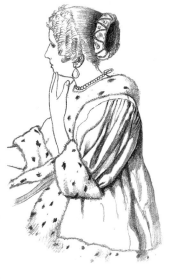

Vermeer's sitter is expensively arrayed in a fabulous jacket of yellow silk and white fur resembling ermine. The tiny wreath around the back of her hair is decorated with pearls and, of course, she has on pearl earrings and necklace. This is just the sort of costume that any artist would enjoy portraying, whatever other charms the sitter might have.

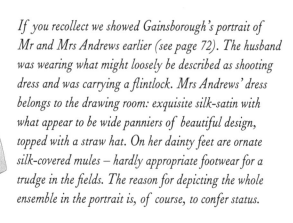

If you recollect we showed Gainsborough's portrait of Mr and Mrs Andrews earlier (see page 72). The husband was wearing what might loosely be described as shooting dress and was carrying a flintlock. Mrs Andrews' dress belongs to the drawing room: exquisite silk-satin with what appear to be wide panniers of beautiful design, topped with a straw hat. On her dainty feet are ornate silk-covered mules – hardly appropriate footwear for a trudge in the fields. The reason for depicting the whole ensemble in the portrait is, of course, to confer status.

The dandified Lord Bernard Stuart, a relative of Charles I, as portrayed by Van Dyck. His exquisite finery obscures the fact that he was also a soldier and keen horseman. The lace and silk cloak and breeches, soft kid gloves and high boots, added to the broad lacy collar and abundant tumbling curly locks, make this a bold statement of aristocratic dash and disdain.

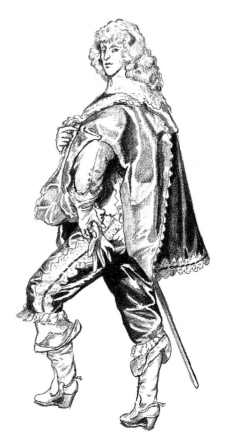

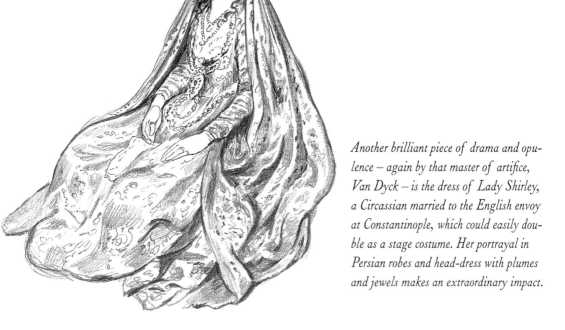

Another brilliant piece of drama and opulence – again by that master of artifice, Van Dyck – is the dress of Lady Shirley, a Circassian married to the English envoy at Constantinople, which could easily double as a stage costume. Her portrayal in Persian robes and head-dress with plumes and jewels makes an extraordinary impact.

Dressing for Character

Some compositional set ups or styles of dress just ask to be drawn, no matter who is the wearer. In these examples we are presented with uncompromising dress of a different kind to that seen in the previous spreads.

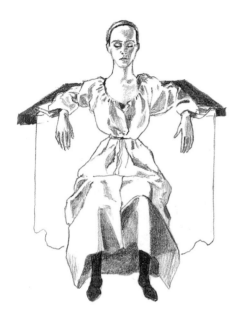

Csorati's Silvana Cerni is wearing a white silk garment that is almost priestly in its plainness. The sitter appears to be meditating or contemplating. Note how the folds in the clothing help to draw attention to her stillness.

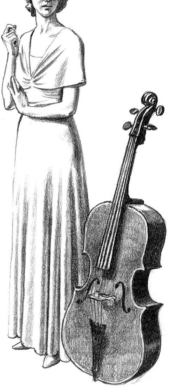

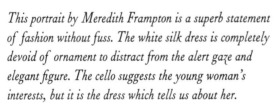

This portrait by Meredith Frampton is a superb statement of fashion without fuss. The white silk dress is completely devoid of ornament to distract from the alert gaze and elegant figure. The cello suggests the young woman's interests, but it is the dress which tells us about her.

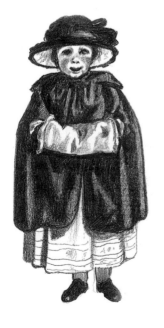

Lady Caroline Scott looks as though she is enjoying wearing this cosy get-up in Reynolds' portrait of her, and was probably much more amenable to posing because of the chance of getting to show off her super clothes. Apparently this infant scion of the aristocracy was also adept at keeping the painter and his friends amused by her chatter.

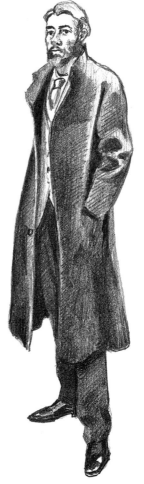

Edward Carpenter, the charismatic Victorian socialist speaker, was drawn and painted by Roger Fry, the Bloomsbury artist. The idea of wearing the overcoat was probably the artist's. He referred to it as 'anarchist' because of the slightly raff-ish air it gave Carpenter, who probably played up this aspect.

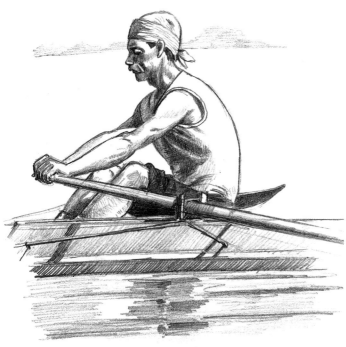

Putting a sitter in sporting kit can be a very good way of giving a portrait extra individuality. John Biglin was an American rower who was drawn and painted by the famous 19th century American artist Thomas Eakins. Biglin's outfit is quite practical and yet it looks almost like fancy dress, especially the dramatic almost piratical scarf around the head.

Head-dress

Head-dress can radically change the appearance of a sitter as well as bring a lot of drama and unusual interest to a portrait. Unless someone wears a hat out of habit or because of their occupation, it is difficult to know beforehand whether it will work in a portrait, but don't be afraid to suggest it because the results can be very impressive. Such an addition can provide insights into character, as these examples show.

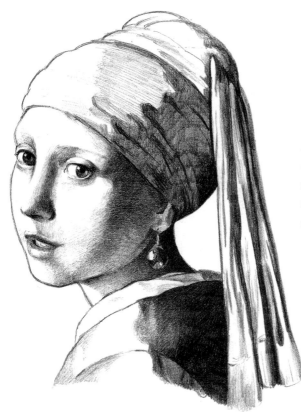

In this copy of Vermeer's famous painting of the girl with the pearl earring, the turban neatly obscures her hair and helps to show off the jewel, which might have been less notice-able if her head was uncovered.

When Vincent Van Gogh was working in the South of France in the late 1880s, he painted a local postman and a young soldier who had befriended him. In both exam-ples their uniform hats lend distinction to faces which are already quite impressive thanks to the drama given them by characterful whiskers.

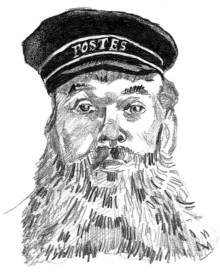

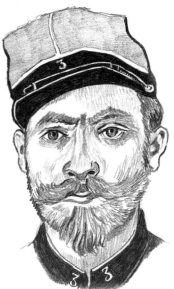

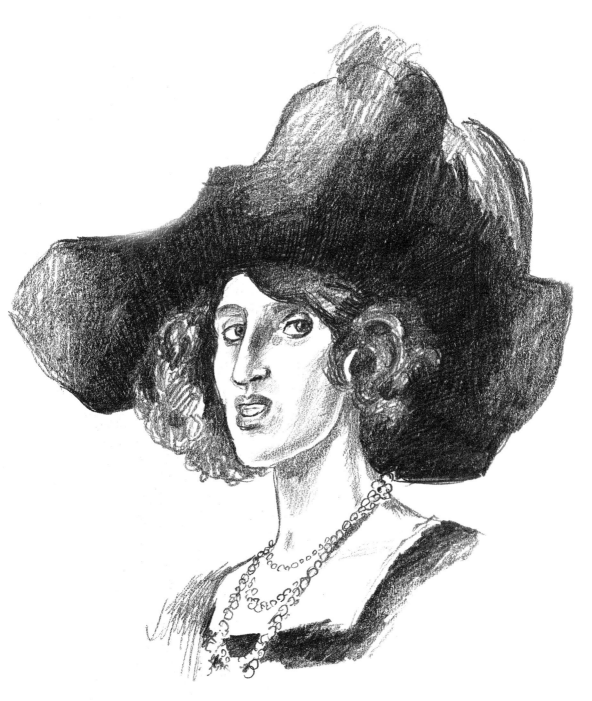

Even by the standards of Edwardian fashion the hat worn by Lady Ottoline Morrell in this copy of a portrait by Augustus John is extraordinary and provides quite a focal point. The art critic of the Manchester Guardian likened the original painting to one of those 'queer ancestral portraits you see in a scene on the stage'. In his biography of John, Michael Holroyd describes the headgear brilliantly as a 'flamboyant topsail of a hat' under which the head is 'held at a proud angle'.

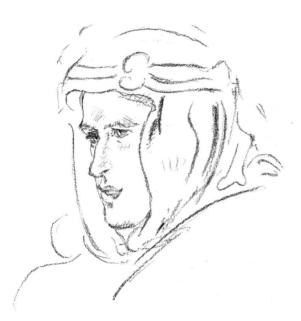

T. E. Lawrence was acting as advisor to
Emir Feisal at the Paris Peace Conference
held at Versailles in 1919 when he was captured in a drawing by Augustus John. A
passionate and active supporter of the Arab
cause, Lawrence wore this style of dress as
a matter of course and not as an affectation.

This extraordinary plumed hat is part of the dress
denoting a Knight of the Order of the Bath. Instead of
following convention and having the head-dress shown
on a table adjacent to him, the 1st Earl of Bellamont
has decided to wear it, perhaps concerned that otherwise
his membership of that august company might be lost on
the viewers of his portrait (after Sir Joshua Reynolds).

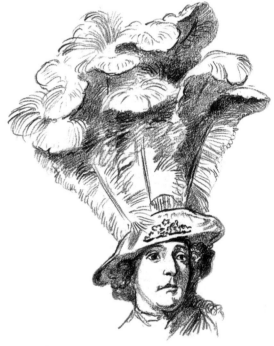

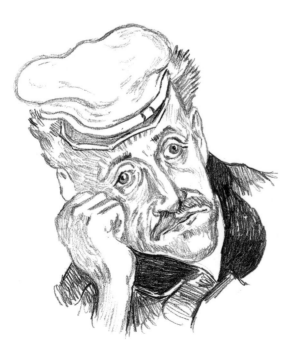

The perky yachting cap sitting atop the head of Dr
Gachet (after Van Gogh) rather contradicts the melancholy expression on his face. Van Gogh remarked of this
portrait: 'Now I have a portrait of Dr Gachet with the
heartbroken expression of our time.'

Hair Styles

Well-dressed hair, especially when the subject is a woman, can add a distinctive air to a portrait. Historically artists have used hair as a means of showing off their own talent as well as enhancing the charm of female sitters. The look of the hair is a great asset in a portrait and should be considered when you arrange to draw someone. Although making it look realistic can be difficult, the texture it adds is worth it.

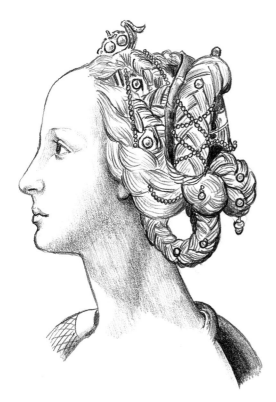

The famous Florentine beauty Simonetta Vespucci, niece of Amerigo Vespucci who gave his name to America, is given tremendous presence in this profile portrait (after Piero di Cosimo), thanks largely to the fantastic jewel-studded plaits looped around her head.

The classical image was all the rage when Pisanello painted the original from which this drawing was made (1433). The hair style is much simpler than Vespucci's but the bandage-like ribbons holding the hair in place serve to accentuate the elegant shape of the young girl's head.

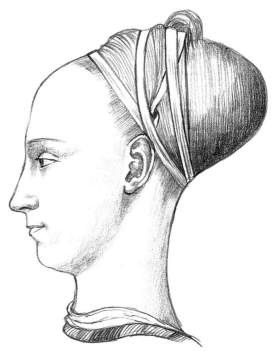

The great masters used the styles of their day to emphasize the femininity of their subjects. Good features can enhance the dramatic effect of elaborate dressing of the hair. However, where the gods have been more sparing in their distribution of looks, artists have to employ more subtle means of portraying their sitters. An elegant hairstyle, assisted by good lighting, can help give substance to the plainest individual.

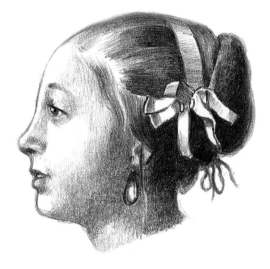

Vermeer used the ribbons and curled hairstyles of the 17th century with great skill to emphasize the femininity of his subjects, as these two examples show.

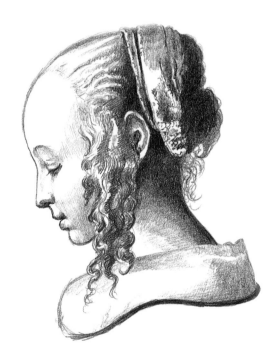

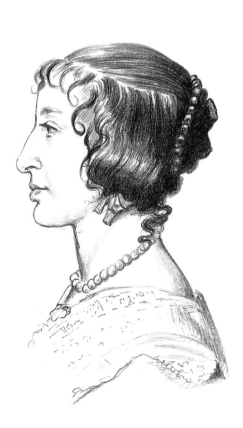

The ribbons and jewellery at this period enabled hair to become an architectural element in portraiture, which artists had to capture by paying attention to the intricacies of the design.

Notice how Van Dyck produces a similar effect to Vermeer with his portrait of Queen Henrietta Maria. Many people when they saw the queen close-to were rather disappointed with her looks, so it is a tribute to Van Dyck's skill that in this profile she appears gracious and elegant.

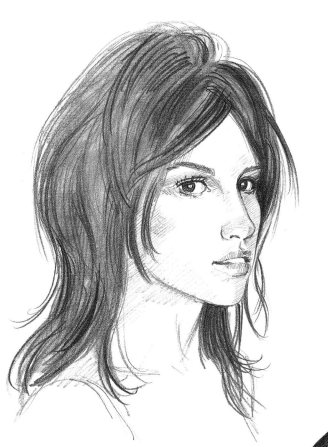

By contrast modern hairstyles are less fussy and less structured than styles from earlier periods. Usually you need only to observe the direction of the combing or, in a more dishevelled look, just allow your pencil, brush or pen to move freely. The direction of the hair is important, but as there is usually less in the way of braiding or curling the problem is simpler.

This example of a modern hairstyle, taken from a fashion magazine promoting hairdressing, gives a seemingly natural look, although this is sometimes attained at some effort and after a great deal of careful work.

Short hair has been very popular with women since the 1920s, and like most modern hairstyles is not difficult to draw.

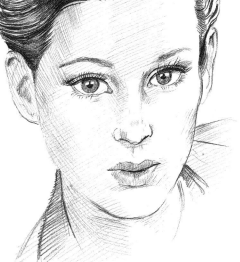

Animals in Portraits

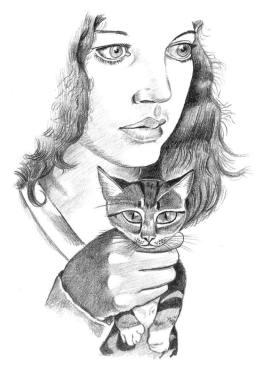

ANIMALS HAVE A PLACE in portraiture simply because so many people are animal-lovers. Historically, horses and dogs have been shown as the natural companions of man. This is especially the case in portraits of leaders. A famous example – already mentioned in this book, on page 70 – is Titian's portrait of the Habsburg Emperor Charles V, who is shown with his faithful hound by his side.

The animals depicted in portraits are not necessarily pets of the people portrayed. Often they are included as symbols or clues to a situation or inner state. Animals as companions and animals as accessories in a painting are usually evident from the arrangement of the portrait. The inclusion of an animal may be partly symbolic – for example, an equestrian portrait of a leader riding a horse – or may be a statement about the character of a person. For example, the inference to be drawn from a picture of a man or woman shown fondling a pet is that this person is sensitive to animals and nature. At different times such symbolic values have been important and have been built into portraits. Sometimes the situation portrayed is much simpler and merely one of the sitter being so fond of the animal that they cannot be shown without their friend. Mostly in these instances there is a distinct element of 'love me-love my pet'.

This brings us to the practical considerations of including animals in portraits. The artist is presented with a difficulty that is different from that involving two or more people. It is easy to get people to take up positions in relation to others for the purpose of drawing them, but impossible to get an animal to do similar, even with training. Keeping the animal still for long enough to enable you to draw it can be a major achievement in itself, and will largely dictate the composition. Always the human part of the equation has to defer to the animal, and this has to be borne in mind when you come to work out a pose.

Organizing the Composition

When it comes to featuring a favourite animal in portraits, art most certainly does mirror life. The golden rule is: animal first, human second. The composition may be agreed between you and the owner but the animal then has to be coaxed into position, preferably one that it can keep long enough for you to make a satisfactory drawing

When the situation is as you want it, draw the animal. Don't worry about the owner at this point, except for making a very rough sketch of the relation between pet and owner. Once you have a good drawing of the animal – and it may take more than one attempt – turn you attention to the owner. If the animal is content to stay put, continue. If it isn't, just put the owner roughly in the pose wanted for the final drawing, without the animal, and carry on.

You can work the two drawings together at this time or later. Obviously it is better if you can progress immediately from drawing the animal to drawing the person, because that will give you a very spontaneous record of the event. If circumstances force you to put the two drawings together afterwards, it is usually better to re-draw the animal in the correct position in relation to the owner rather than redraw the owner. The reason for this is that a portrait of an animal is much easier to reproduce in a second drawing than the human being because the animal's expression is unlikely to change.

It can be very helpful – and in some circumstances essential – to make a photographic record of the animal. Certainly it is easier to draw an animal from photos than it is a human being.

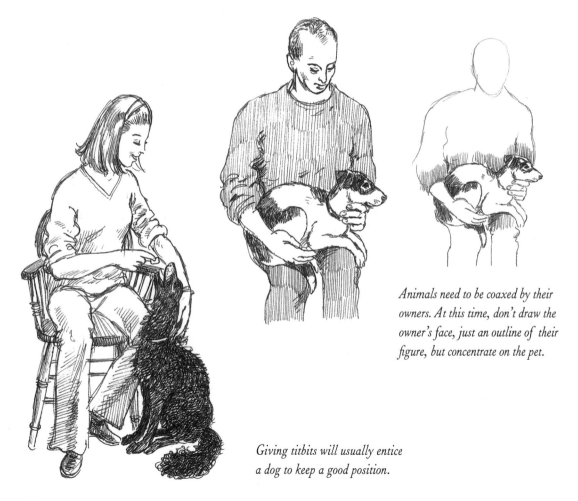

Animals need to be coaxed by their owners. At this time, don't draw the owner's face, just an outline of their figure, but concentrate on the pet.

Giving titbits will usually entice a dog to keep a good position.

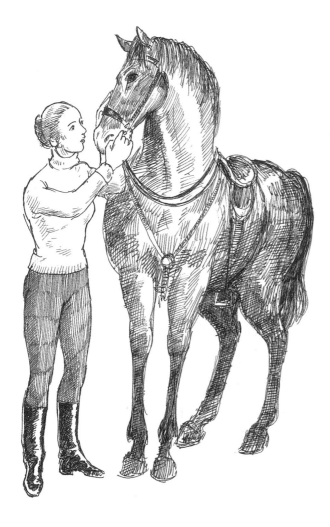

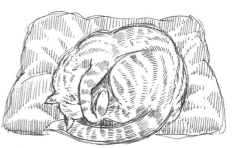

Cats are easier to draw when they are asleep and unaware of your studying gaze on them.

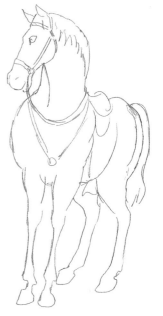

If you are portraying a horse you will probably need several attempts to find a good position in relation to the owner. Some horses are very twitchy and will only stand still when they are in their stall, where it is very difficult to get a good view of them. Photography can come to the rescue in these circumstances.

When you have positioned the animal and drawn it (top right), the drawing of the owner can go ahead. Take into account the position of the animal and link your sitter with it, perhaps by using a mock-up, as in our example (right). After you've tried this several times, the composition will begin to look more natural.

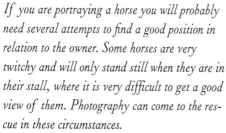

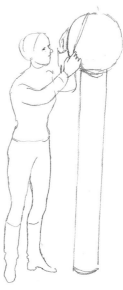

143

Man's Best Friends

What you cannot guarantee when drawing animals in portraits is the animal staying in position for any length of time, even if it is well trained. Dogs and horses are the most amenable to posing, especially dogs, which is probably why historically they feature so heavily in animal portraiture. In the 18th century the inclusion of dogs and horses underlined the importance of country life and pursuits to the ruling elite. It could also provide opportunities for telling us something about the character of the sitter.

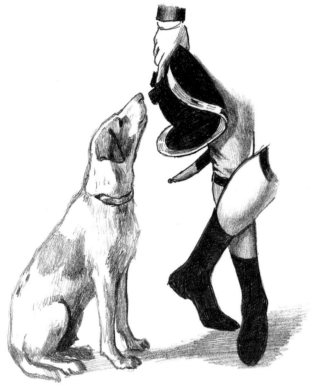

After Gainsborough's portrait of an officer of the 4th Regiment of Foot (1776) – this is not such a difficult arrangement to draw, because a dog will sit for a while, but the head would have to be drawn separately, probably with someone holding his head in position.

After Gainsborough's portrait of Henry, Duke of Buccleuch (1770). The most difficult aspect of this rather touching portrait is drawing the shapes so the dog doesn't come across as just a hairy mass. The details of his coat are very important, and for an animal as furry as this one you should expect to make several sketches of how the hairs lie in order to get it right.

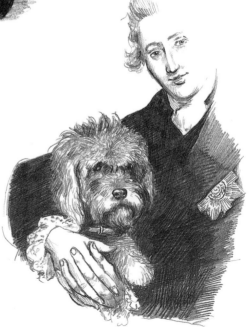

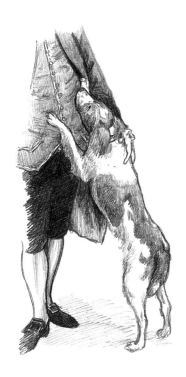

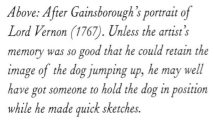

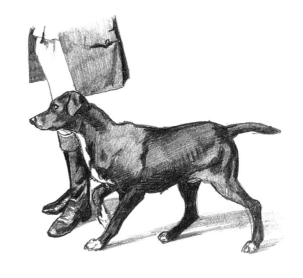

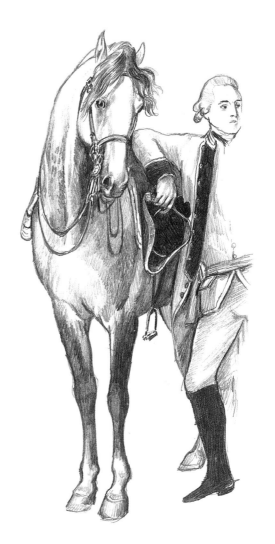

Above: After Gainsborough's portrait of Lord Vernon (1767). Unless the artist's memory was so good that he could retain the image of the dog jumping up, he may well have got someone to hold the dog in position while he made quick sketches.

Top right: After Stubbs' portrait of Sir John Nelthorpe (1776). Stubbs had extensive knowledge of anatomy and it can be assumed that he put it to good use in his animal paintings. In the absence of a camera, you would have to spend many hours observing to achieve this degree of verisimilitude.

Right: Ostensibly a portrait of Edward, Viscount Ligonier, by Gainsborough (1771), the most telling comment made about the original was that it was a 'portrait of a damn fine horse, with adjacent human, proving the superiority of the animal to the man'.

145

Woman's Best Friends

In many Western societies the family pet has always been treated more like a member of the family than a mere animal. Since the 18th century the association of a human being with an animal in a portrait has been seen as a sign of sensitivity to the condition of species other than our own, and also as a demonstration of the sitter's good character. There can be a danger of sentimentality creeping in, but this is easily prevented by taking an honest, objective approach to the portrait and allying it to sound technique.

In one of the best dog portraits of the 20th century, by Lucian Freud, the artist's first wife, Kitty, is shown with a white bull terrier cuddling up to her lap. The original was painted in tempera, a very meticulous method where you use a brush almost like a pencil, and so lends itself to depiction in pencil, as here. The portrait is really of Freud's wife but the dog is so clearly defined that it almost takes over the picture. The only way that the human model keeps the attention is because she has bared one breast and has enormous luminous eyes. Hundreds of tiny strokes were necessary to capture the dog's smooth but hairy coat for this copy.

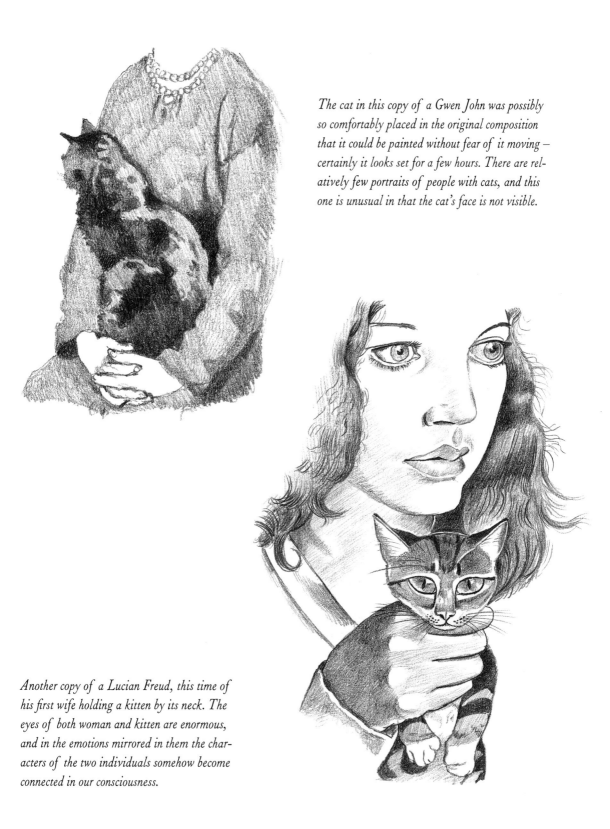

The cat in this copy of a Gwen John was possibly so comfortably placed in the original composition that it could be painted without fear of it moving – certainly it looks set for a few hours. There are relatively few portraits of people with cats, and this one is unusual in that the cat's face is not visible.

Another copy of a Lucian Freud, this time of his first wife holding a kitten by its neck. The eyes of both woman and kitten are enormous, and in the emotions mirrored in them the characters of the two individuals somehow become connected in our consciousness.

Furniture and Props

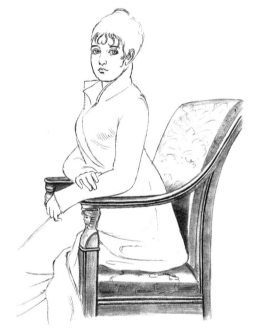

BECAUSE OF ITS NATURE, portraiture usually involves the use of furniture, props or the special arrangement of a place to produce a satisfying end result. It is possible, of course, to set a portrait out-of-doors where there is little if any furniture, but even in this environment it is necessary to allow the person to become 'the sitter' and include external visual clues that are expressive of character or situation. In many simple head-and-shoulders portraits you will find some evidence of place purposely included to add to the overall effect.

It might be your idea to draw a subject in their home, posing them in a favourite armchair in their sitting room. This can be a powerful way of presenting a person, but is also very time-consuming because it necessitates making very good drawings of everything in sight. A good way of managing this approach is to set up the surrounds, draw them and then tackle your subject separately. For the final drawing you marry the two elements by drawing the person onto your drawing of the surrounds.

The most common adjuncts can vary enormously in type and character, and which you choose to include can dramatically alter the mood or message conveyed. Don't always choose the most comfortable piece of furniture to pose your subject in or around. Sometimes a more spartan item can inject a welcome tension in a portrait.

Nor does a subject's habitual pose necessarily give the best portrait, as the story of how the photographer Karsh obtained his famous shot of Winston Churchill demonstrates. Churchill was sitting with his trademark large cigar in his mouth, looking contented and not at all as Karsh wanted to show him. The photographer was after a more truculent look that would reflect his subject's defiance of the recently defeated Nazi regime. Just before taking his shot, Karsh reached over and took the cigar out of Churchill's mouth. The expression on the statesman's face was the making of a very powerful portrait. The moral: Develop strategies that help deliver the result you want.

Using the Chair as a Prop

The conventions of using furniture in portraits has not changed dramatically over the centuries, as the similarities between the following examples show.

Sitting back to front on a chair was as popular in the 17th century as it is in modern portraiture. Furniture is not sacrosanct. Use it to your advantage.

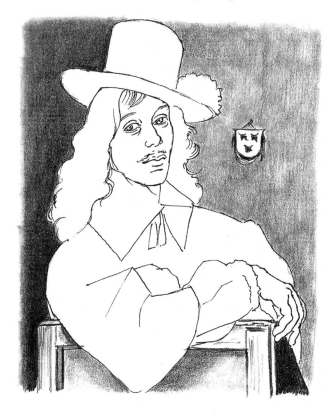

Frans Hals' dandified subject, Willem Coyman, seems very aware of having his portrait painted. The pose of arm resting very lightly across the back of the chair gets across the rather insouciant quality of the sitter. Coyman's social pedigree is pointed up by the family coat of arms hanging on the back wall.

The picture of Pete Postlethwaite by Christopher Thompson shows a similar view to that of the Dutch gentleman. The chair has more of a presence here and its use is an interesting mixture of casual and confrontational, the black inner panel looking out at us contrasting with the actor's sombre averted gaze.

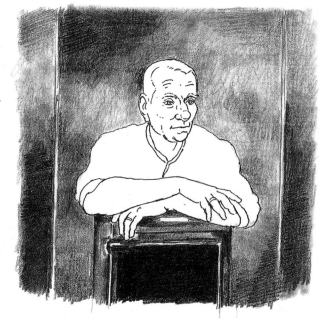

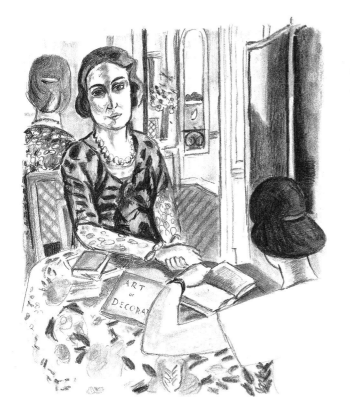

In this copy of Matisse's painting of Baroness Gourgaud, the artist was aiming to produce a decorative painting in which the portrait is just another element of décor. The baroness seems to be sitting in her own home, on the table in front of her are books and papers on art or decoration, and she is being read to. In fact, the portrait was painted at Cannes, in the Hotel Carlton. The other woman is the model Henriette Davricarrere, who Matisse insisted on having in the picture. Matisse disliked painting portraits except on his own terms. The patterned tablecloth, the hands of the figures placed in close proximity, the decorative effect of the screen, the view into the next room, the view out of the window and the mirror image all add up to a decorative painting that just happens to be a portrait too.

This copy of 'Mum' by Benjamin Sullivan (2002) shows a room in the artist's house, judging by the brushes in jam jars on the mantelpiece and the paint on the bare boards. However, the chandeliers and round converse mirror on the wall behind the sitter remind us of Van Eyck's portrait of the Arnolfini marriage (see pages 168–69), as does the extreme tilt of the floor's perspective. The armchair with tartan rug thrown over it might have made a more comfortable perch than the hard kitchen chair she is sitting on, but it would not have contributed the edge that comes out in the woman's direct gaze. The bookshelves on either side of the chimney-breast help to give space, tone and texture to the background so that the final result looks like a working portrait and not especially posed. The table in the foreground with its opened crisp packet adds a touch of almost humorous texture to the portrait.

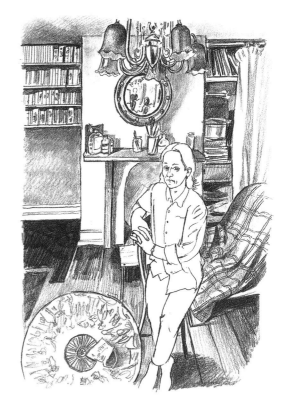

Mirror Images

Reflecting a view of a sitter in a mirror is a device that many artists have used, sometimes repeatedly. Although by taking this approach you have to produce two drawings for the price of one, the effect achieved is very often worth the extra effort. Somehow the viewer comes across as being more involved and the method offers opportunities for the artist to include additional information to the benefit of the finished picture. Quite apart from bringing an intriguing quality to a portrait, this approach can also add depth.

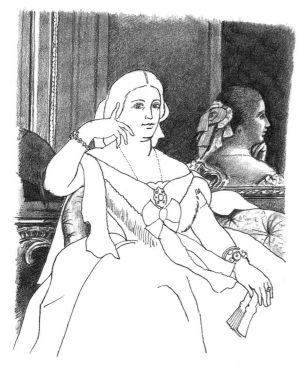

Ingres seated his subject, Mme Moitessier (1856), on a chaise longue and placed the mirror behind, enabling us to see her both from the front and in profile.

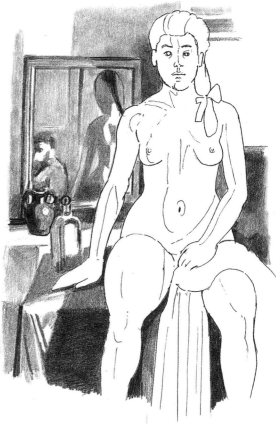

For his portrait of Carmeline (1903), Matisse introduced an interesting variation on a theme he used several times in his work. The model's back is strongly reflected in the mirror and beside it we see the artist himself, painting his sitter. This device greatly increases the immediacy of the portrait.

Bare Necessities

The function of furniture and props in portraits has always been to contribute to the effect. In the past this was often achieved by including many elements in the composition, all of which contributed in some way to the end result. Reducing these elements to a bare minimum and including hardly any background can have just as much impact, as the following examples demonstrate.

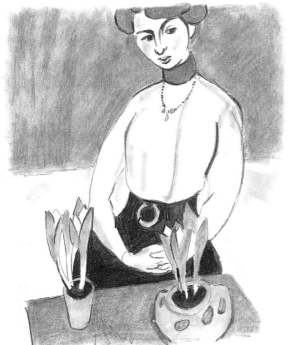

In Matisse's portrait of Jeanne Vaderin (1910) the girl and the tulips in the two pots are similar in terms of shape, and both could be said to be in the first flush of youth. Matisse was interested in the idea of making the human and plant forms in a picture reflect the same quality, and here, as in the earlier portrait of Baroness Gourgaud, all of the elements, including props, furniture and Jeanne herself, are schemes of decoration rather than objects portrayed in their own right.

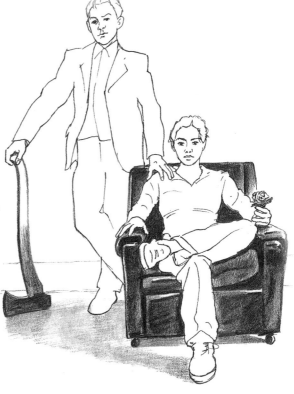

The double portrait of Mr David Frankel and Miss Grace Ayson by Gavin Edmonds (2001) incorporates very little in the way of furniture apart from a leather chair on which Miss Ayson is sitting. The contrast between the black chair and the white floor and wall behind it maximizes the dramatic effect, as do the poses of the two figures. The props they are holding are at extremes in terms of their symbolism: an axe and a rose. The black and white dress of both participants is also uncompromising.

Spatial Awareness

These images demonstrate variations on a setting where the sitter is placed in a space that seems to define something about him. As you will notice, the way the space is inhabited has a very different effect.

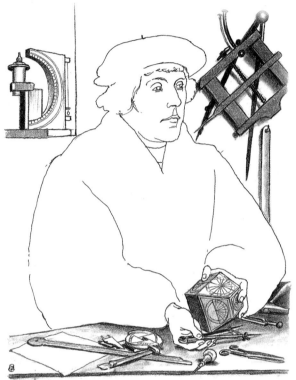

In 'The Astronomer' by Holbein (1528) the subject is surrounded by the elements of his science. His desk is covered with the tools that he works with, and on the wall behind are more astronomical instruments. The props in this example give us obvious clues to the man's identity and his profession. At this time there was prestige in being identified as an astronomer but also a risk because of the antipathy of the Church towards science.

Cezanne has placed the writer Gustave Geffroy at his desk, surrounded by books, his writing materials and a few personal mementos (1895). He looks completely at home, in his element, whereas we, the viewers, are kept at arm's length by the furniture and the props which act as a barrier.

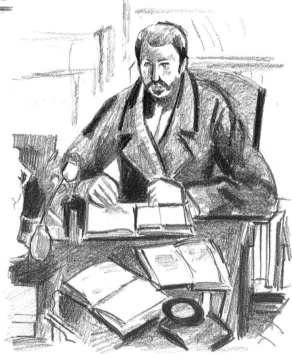

'Eddie' by Jason Butler (2002) makes use of a plain hard chair set forthrightly in the artist's bleak studio with the subject sitting four square, hands on knees, bare feet resting on his shoes. The sitter is very exposed to the viewer but still in a way isolated by the space around him. He is not in his element or at ease, a feeling that is accentuated by the cup of coffee balancing on his knee.

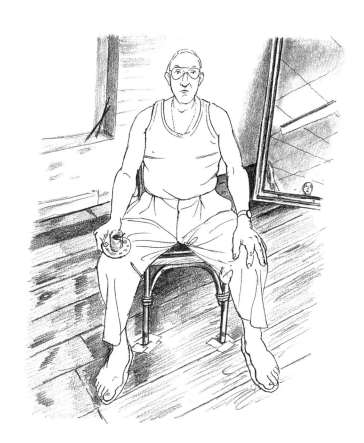

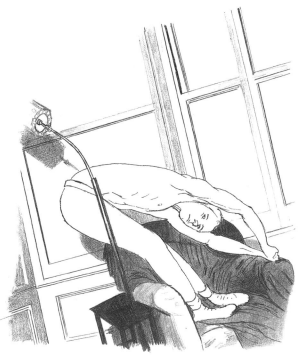

This extraordinary portrait by Philip Hale (2002) makes very unusual use of furniture and the human figure and is not what one would immediately think of when setting up a portrait. The title – 'The Male Imperative to Assert while the Female is Content to Remain Submissive' – suggests that this is a satirical portrait, because the young man in the picture is practically standing on his head to produce an unusual effect. The interior of the room angled at several degrees and the subject standing bent double on an armchair alongside a standard lamp produces disorienting juxtapositions.

Active and Passive Partners

Even the most unlikely pieces of furniture or most mundane objects can be used to create interest in a portrait. Props to produce a setting for a portrait are usually made to look as natural as possible in order to convince the viewer that this is how the artist found the subject when drawn. If they do their work well the result looks natural but provides information to help us connect with the subject. Of course, sometimes props are just incidental and act merely as aesthetic devices to round off the shape or colour of the portrait, but nevertheless do their job.

A useful rule is not to include anything that takes too much attention from the face. Having a prop as a focal point can be a good idea, but it should never be allowed to upstage the main participant. In these examples we find props playing a variety of roles to varying degrees, either as indications of narrative or as symbolic devices.

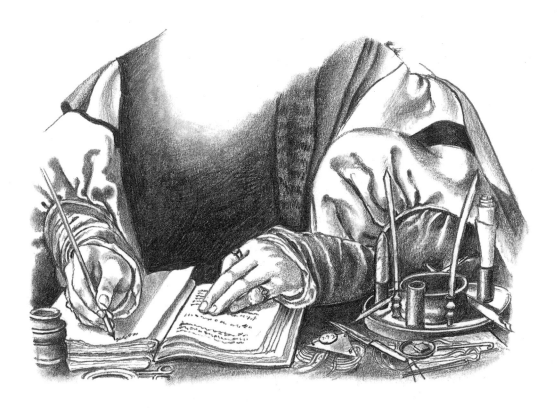

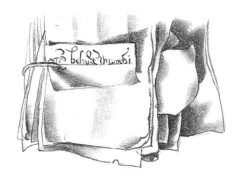

This copy of Jan Gossaert's portrait of a Flemish banker (1530) shows him at his desk writing. Around him are quill pens, inkwell, penknife, paper etc, all that he needs for writing bank drafts, account loans and bills, some of which are suspended on the wall behind him, tied up in bunches (right).

In the 16th century, when François Clouet painted the original of this portrait, a bathroom setting was very fashionable. The bath was not an ordinary daily ablution but a special event at which quite a few people would be present. The soft silk cloth draped inside the bath of this gentlewoman was to ensure that her skin would not be abraided by the rough wooden or woven surface of the tub. Remember, this is long before the introduction of smooth coatings for baths. The draped material to her left is a rather theatrical device, hinting perhaps that what is a private action has become public.

The sitter is thought to be Diane de Poitiers, mistress of Henri II, although there have been other attributions, including Mary, Queen of Scots.

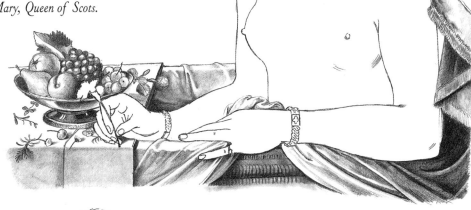

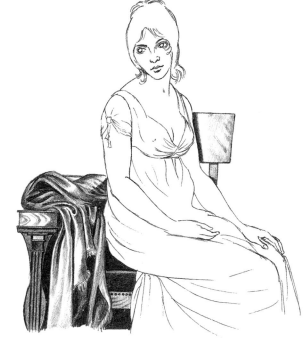

If a portrait lacks background detail it stands to reason that any furniture will take on more significance. The neo-classical painter Jacques Louis David used this lack, together with sharply defined lighting, to increase the focus on his sitters. The original of this portrait of a young girl is by a follower of David who has copied the master's approach. The sideways position on the chair increases the informality of the pose, as does the shawl casually thrown on the table behind her.

Settings with a History

Historic characters have a built-in list of props that could be used to show their importance. The modern portraitist has to try to emulate this example by working out which objects will enhance the history of his subject. If your subject has done something celebrated, you need to show what this was. The achievements of sportsmen, scientists, artists and soldiers are relatively easy to convey visually. More difficult are those of politicians, local worthies and businessmen, and their portraits have to be approached with great imagination.

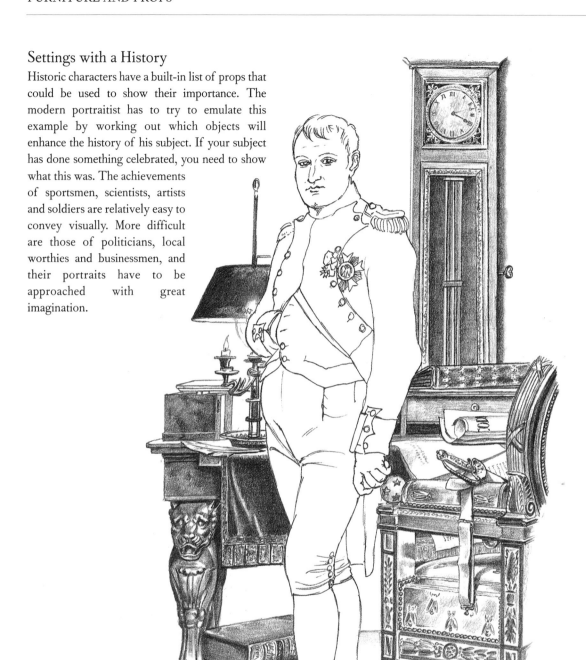

Napoleon was said to have been very pleased with the original of this portrait of himself by Jacques Louis David (1812). The furniture and props have been carefully manipulated to get across the message of the Emperor's dedication. The hands of the clock are pointing to past four and the candles in the desk lamp have burnt down. Unrolled on the desk is the cause of his toil-ing through the night – the Code Napoleon. The Emperor's sword is shown nearby, inferring that his role as defender of the French nation is not being neglected as a consequence. When shown the finished work, Napoleon said that 'the French people could see that their Emperor was labouring for their laws during the night and giving them "la gloire" by day.'

Doña Teresa Sureda *was the wife of a close friend of the artist Goya and sat for the original of this portrait after the two men had enjoyed a night out on the town. It is said that in posing her in an uncomfortably large armchair, Goya was getting his own back for her complaint that he was a bad influence on her husband. Certainly she looks very stiff and reproachful, but whether this was due to the chair or her attitude to Goya it is impossible to surmise.*

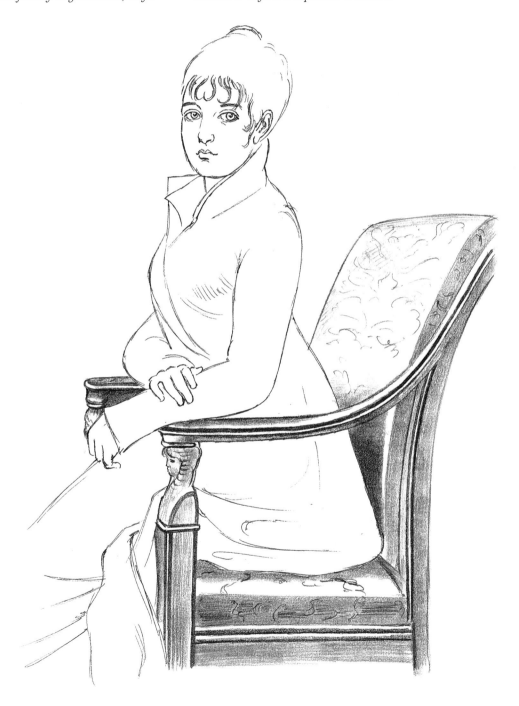

Symbolism

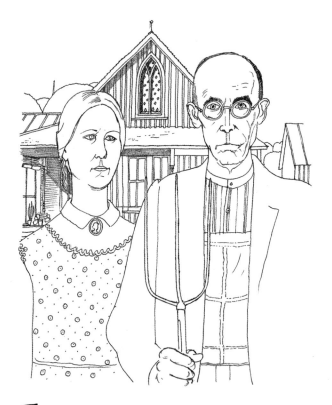

*I*N ALL PICTURES there is some element of symbolism. In portraits these symbols are often quite subtly incorporated to highlight the identity of the sitter and tell the viewer something about them. Best clothes or official garments are very obvious symbolic devices, as are specific objects placed to evoke the history or background of the sitter. In fact, look at any portrait closely and you will find everything in it will stand for some aspect of the sitter's life, profession or character.

Much of the symbolism is on a psychological level. The expression that comes across the face of a subject when he or she is not engaging with others or something is as much a symbol as the type of dress worn or pose adopted. An expression can symbolize the inner being, although it is not always seen as such by the casual viewer and may go unnoticed if that viewer knows nothing about the subject. However, when you place an object in a sitter's hand or beside his elbow, instantly you are making an allusion to some connection beyond the life of the picture. The artist can work on such devices to point up a particular quality of the sitter or just refer to some part of his or her way of life.

The use of symbols was much more widespread in portraits from earlier ages when there was a well understood vocabulary of iconography centred on social class and position. Symbolism is still relevant and is still used in modern portraits but less obviously. Nowadays it is more personal and harder to define on a social level. Gone are the days when portraits were littered with clues that could be easily interpreted.

When you try to give symbolic significance to your own drawings you will find it hard to do so without taking a somewhat formal approach. However, if you can incorporate symbols in a subtle way, you will find them adding a great deal of interest to your portraits.

Social Mores

Symbolism can be used to tell truths about society, individuals or a situation. The way the artist chooses to portray these truths will be down to his style and personal approach to drawing, as the following examples show. A good artist will make his values clear in his work, even if he has to present them in code, which is what symbolism provides, as the following examples demonstrate.

Kasimir Malevitch was one of the leading exponents of Suprematism, an unrelenting geometric form of abstract painting that was popular in artistic circles in Russia soon after the Revolution. However, with the rise of Stalin and the beginnings of the official Social-Realistic school of art, Malevitch's abstract ideals were suppressed as non-Communist. When Malevitch painted the original of this portrait of his wife, he was contravening two of the main rules laid down for artists by the Soviet authorities. First, that a personal relationship should not form the basis of a painting (this was considered bourgeois); and secondly, that abstractionism was not an acceptable means of expression.

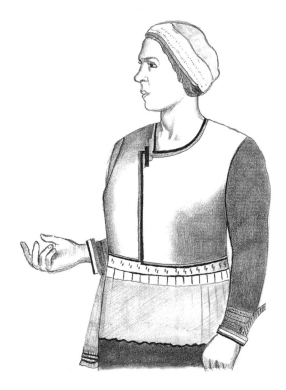

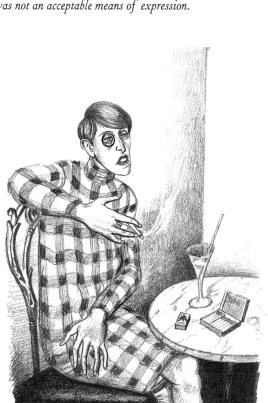

For artist Otto Dix, the journalist Sylvia von Harden epitomizes the new emancipated woman emerging in Germany after 1918. She is shown behaving as a worldly intellectual, cigarette expressively in hand as she holds forth. The cocktail and the style of table and chair hint at café society, a milieu in which she is obviously at ease. Although well turned out, she makes no concession to male notions of femininity: note the bobbed hair, monocle screwed tightly into eye, and unrevealing dress. However the glimpse of stocking top and garter suggests that her type of woman is as sexually liberated as she is free of concern about the opinion of men.

In this copy of 'The Meeting' or 'Have a nice day, Mr Hockney', Peter Blake is parodying Gustave Courbet's painting, 'Bonjour, Monsieur Courbet' (1854) with his revolutionary Pop-art effects. Courbet showed himself walking across country with his painter's gear on his back, being greeted respectfully by his friend and patron. In its artless composition the painting challenged the very posed norms of academic art. In his punning take on the Courbet,

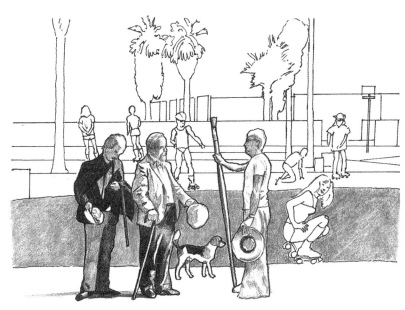

Blake places himself at the centre of the image with Harry Geldzahler, David Hockney's main patron in California, standing deferentially behind him and Hockney himself on the right. Hockney is shown holding a gigantic paint brush in his right hand. Around the three men we see roller skaters in functional dress against a background of modern buildings and palm trees.

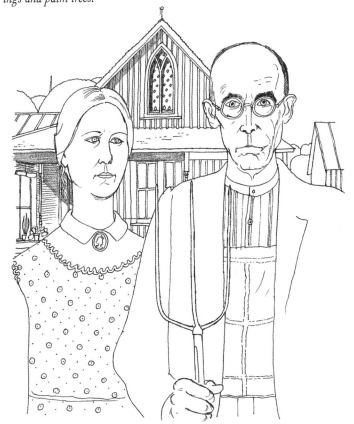

The American realist painter Grant Wood used a careful craftsmanlike style to imbue his images with a strong formal element. The couple of Mid-Westerners portrayed in 'American Gothic' symbolize the uprightness and friendly home-making attitudes that made the infant United States such an attractive place for immigrants. The composition is direct and uncompromising although we see in these people both kindness and humanity.

Royal is as Royal Does

Symbolism has always been used as a vehicle for reinforcing the images of the powerful. Absolute monarchy became a hot topic in the 17th century, especially in England where it cost a king (Charles I) his head. Here we see two very different depictions of kingship, each reflecting political reality.

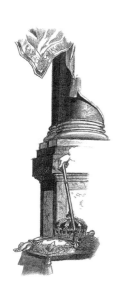

The double column of Roman design suggests stability and power.

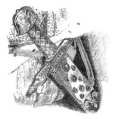

The jewelled sword from a different age suggests continuity of the monarchy.

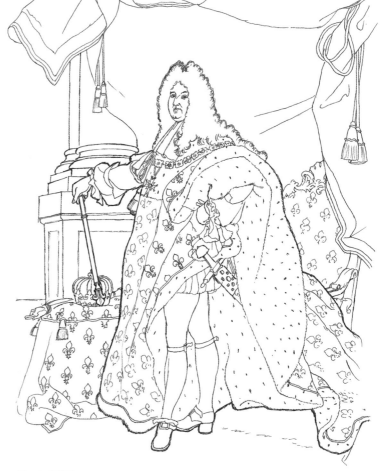

Hyacinth Rigaud depicts the Sun King, Louis XIV, as the personification of absolute monarchy. The haughty pose, flamboyant but with a distancing quality, declares the monarch's position of supremacy within the state. The showing of the king's legs was traditional in full-length portraits of monarchy in this period, and the hand on hip depicts aristocratic concern. The drapes hanging above and to his right allude, rather theatrically, to the monarchy's central role in the politics of France and Europe. The extraordinary gesture of holding the sceptre upside down, like a walking stick, shows that the king is above showing the respect that is normally paid to such an important badge of office. The ermine-lined robe trailing across the dais covered in fleur-de-lys – the emblem of French monarchy – further emphasizes his unequalled status. Every gesture, object and material in this portrait is a symbol of the regal power of the king of France. Finally, he is shown wearing a periwig of the latest design, inferring that the French king creates the fashion that lesser monarchs copy later.

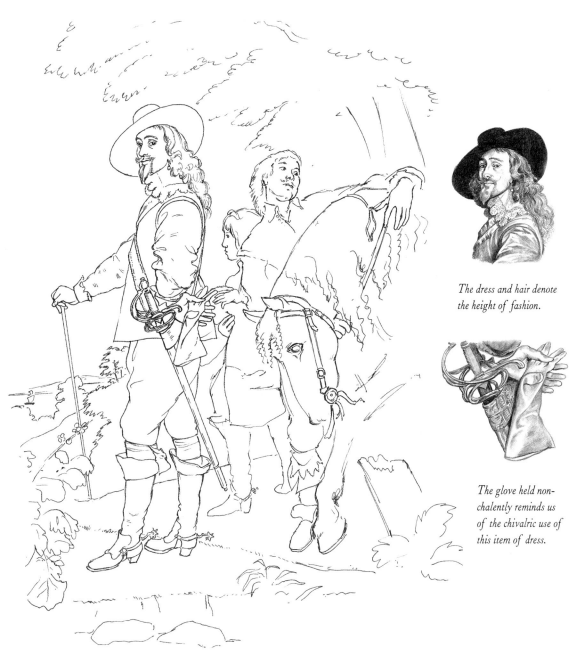

The dress and hair denote the height of fashion.

The glove held nonchalently reminds us of the chivalric use of this item of dress.

Typical English understatement has gone into this portrait of Charles I by Anthony Van Dyck. The set-up is similar to that for Louis XIV but the symbolism is certainly more subdued, as you would expect from a monarchy under attack. The English king was not as powerful as his continental neighbour and here he is shown dressed as a cavalier, devoid of the paraphernalia of state. However, his royal status is underlined by the pose –
hand on hip, walking stick held almost as a sceptre, the cool, haughty appraising look. The attendance of a groom and a page carrying a coat or blanket for the king's pleasure, and the horse's gesture almost of obeisance, suggest this is more than a portrayal of a country gentleman. Van Dyck was an expert at making the apparent casualness of the setting into a statement of symbolic power and elegance.

Pictures of Virtue

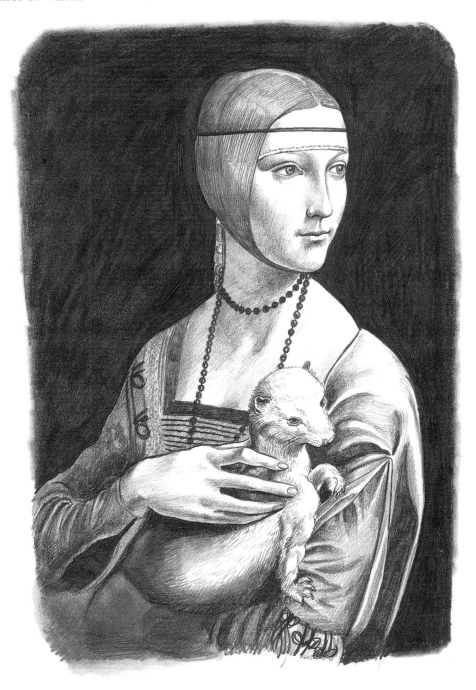

Leonardo's portrait of Cecilia Gallerani, the young mistress, later wife, of Ludovico Sforza, Duke of Milan, shows her in a sweetly informal pose. The averted gaze and plain arrangement of her hair denote respectability.

The ermine she holds echoes her youthful, sinuous grace. A symbol of purity, the animal also represents a pun on her name which would not have been lost on Renaissance minds; 'Gale' in Greek means ermine.

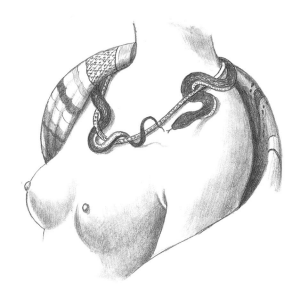

The portrait of the great Florentine beauty Simonetta Vespucci, reputedly mistress of Giuliano de'Medici, has already been seen in the section on clothing and hairstyles (see page 137), where her extraordinarily complex hair braiding and jewellery had in themselves symbolic presence in showing off the almost fairy-tale princess. The portrait was done after her death in remembrance of her beauty. The snake coiling around her neck and shoulders is an effective symbol of the cancer that carried her off. However, there is a suggestion that the snake is about to bite its own tail, in which case it could double as a symbol of eternity, and the portrait could read as a way of keeping alive Simonetta's beauty.

Marie de Valengin was the daughter of Philip the Good, Grand Duke of Burgundy. Undoubtedly elegant, as befits her status, there is a hint of religiosity about the way she has been portrayed, especially in the downward gaze, folded hands and the arrangement of her veil. However, as well as incorporating these symbols of her virtue, Rogier van der Weyden shows us other aspects too, suggesting her fullness of spirit in the sensuous mouth and the glowing countenance.

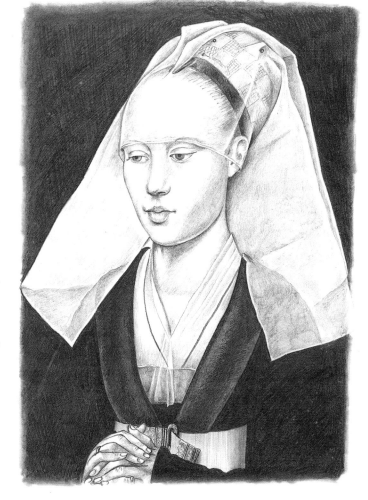

Making the Most of the Mundane

The symbolism in Jan Van Eyck's 'Arnolfini Marriage' (1434) is so complex that art historians are still unsure of the meaning attaching to some of the picture's content. It is quite certain, however, that the original represents both a blessing and a legal affirmation of the union of the couple portrayed, thought to be Giovanni Arnolfini and Giovanna Cenami. Every movement, position and object in this room underlines the theme of marriage. It is, in effect, a marriage contract produced by an artist.

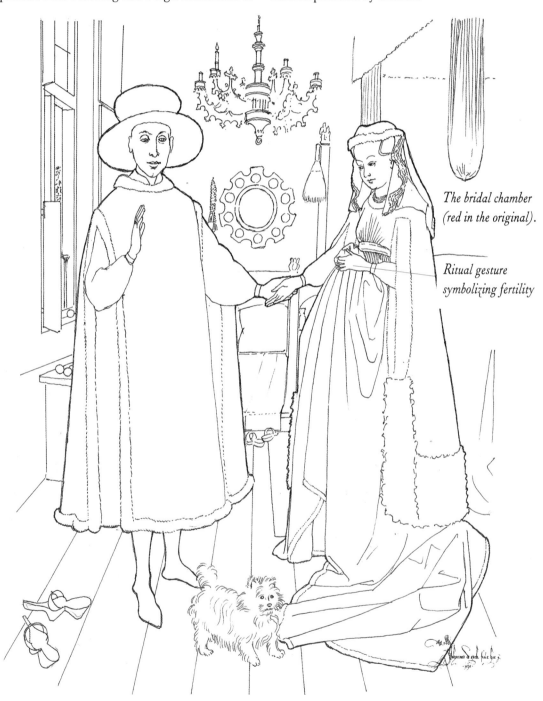

The bridal chamber (red in the original).

Ritual gesture symbolizing fertility

The single wedding candle burning in the chandelier cites traditional Annunciation iconography.

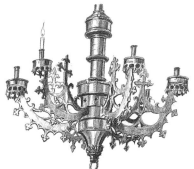

The 'immaculate mirror' (speculum sine macula) signifies the purity of the Virgin and the bride. In the mirror, which is surrounded by scenes from the Passion, you can see two figures, one the artist and a second witness to the marriage.

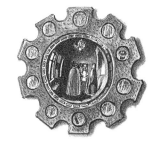

The brush is a pun on Virgo/Virga to emphasize virgin purity, as well as an allusion to the 'rod of life', symbol of masculine fertility and strength; bridegrooms were ritually beaten with a switch to ensure couples were blessed with large numbers of children.

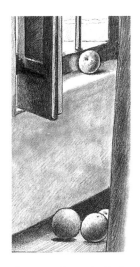

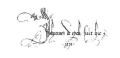

Van Eyck signed the painting as a witness, giving it the legitimacy of a legal document.

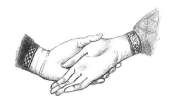

Promising marriage without the presence of a priest was customary in the 15th century by the joining of hands. The pledge was considered legally binding. The bridegroom holds his other hand up very deliberately. He may be about to place it over the bride's open palm or perhaps make the sign of the Cross.

Fruit alludes to the Fall and warns against sinful behaviour. The light coming through the window suggests that the ceremony is taking place under the eye of the Creator.

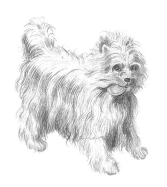

The dog is a symbol of devotion and conjugal fidelity.

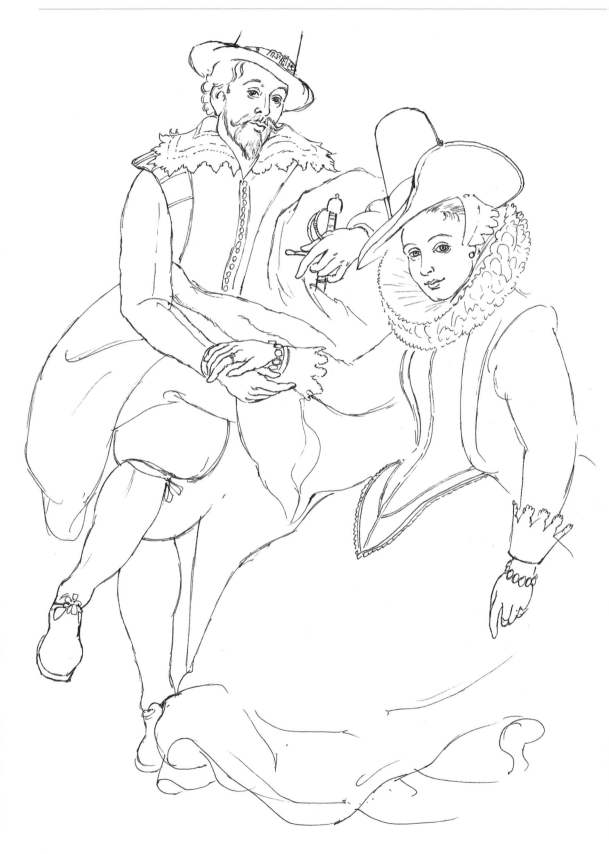

Portrait of a Marriage

Like Van Eyck's double portrait of Arnolfini and his bride, this example is also a statement about marriage, although one that is perhaps more agreeable to our eyes. In Peter Paul Rubens' depiction of himself and his new wife Isabella Brant (1609), we see not so much a declaration of intent as one of fact. Isabella was the daughter of a rich aristocrat and probably came from a better family than her spouse. Rubens was not only a great painter with access to the courts of Europe but also a diplomat with very good connections.

The beautiful embroidery on her bodice and the extravagant ruff she wears, with the precious bracelets around her wrists, give a festive wedding appearacnce to the couple.

The tone of tender familiarity and equality is one we recognize. The pose is not so far away from how a modern couple might present themselves for a portrait celebrating their union. She kneels on the ground, her hand in his, but there is no hint of subservience, only of loving attention flowing between them.

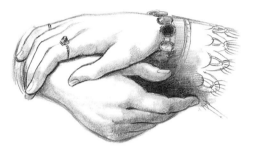

The joining of the hands is, as we have already seen, a symbol of a pledge of marriage. Here the interpretation can be broadened, for these two are already man and wife. The way the hands are joined tells us that this is a contract based on love, not commerce. The couple's open, almost joyous, expressions support this idea.

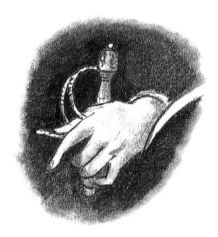

The placement of Rubens' hand on the hilt of his sword implies that he has aristocratic credentials, if not by birth then certainly by achievement.

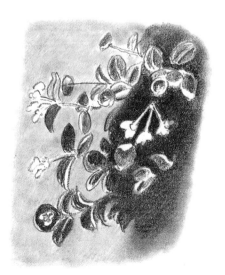

In the original the couple are seated outside in a garden with honeysuckle growing in the bushes around and behind them, giving us an intimation of the honeymoon. Plants are typically used in art to symbolize the pastoral idyll of the garden of paradise.

Elements of Symbolism

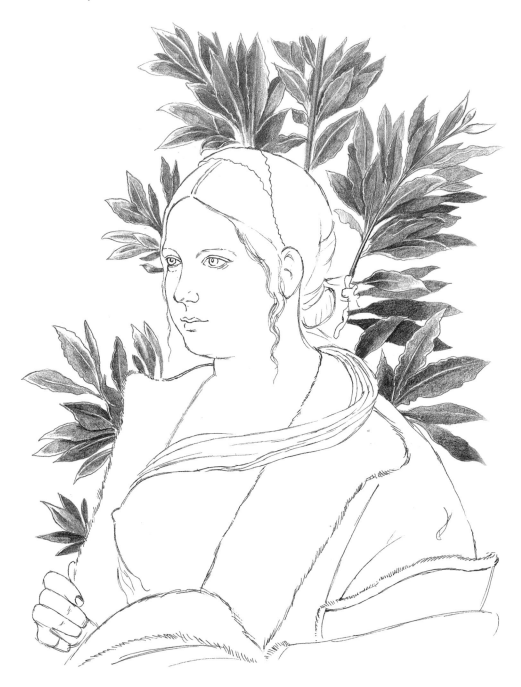

Laura was the great beloved and muse of the Italian poet Petrarch. In this copy of Giorgone's depiction of her (1506), her identity is underlined by the laurel bush shown behind her head and shoulders. The laurel was given by Apollo and the Muses to crown the great poets of antiquity. The actual model for this portrait may have been a muse for Giorgione or a patron. The veil suggests a bridal portrait and the bared breast refers to Amazonian chastity.

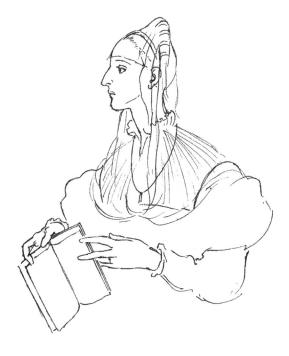

Laura Battiferri was considered an 'incarnation of chaste and noble beauty'. In this sketch after Agnolo Bronzino's dramatic portrait (1555), various symbols are included which tell us about the sitter and spell out her importance. A connection is made to her namesake, Petrarch's Laura, and as Battiferri herself was an intellectual we can only assume she would have approved of this identification.

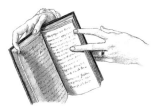

The hand with its outspread fingers indicates a Petrarch sonnet to Laura, with whom the sitter probably identifies.

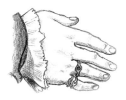

The gesture of hand on heart denotes sincerity.

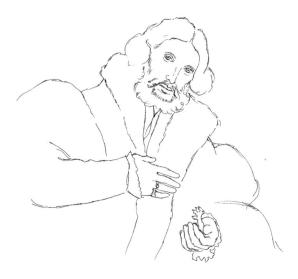

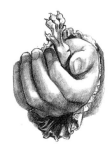

'Recognize the lion by its paw' is a motto of classical writers.

The 16th-century painter Lorenzo Lotto often used symbolic gestures and objects in his portraits. This next example ('Man with Golden Paw', 1527) presents us with a series of puzzles. We have no idea who the man is, why he is holding a paw or what the paw means. It might simply stand for a gift of strength, or it might be the emblem of a particular family. Among the many guesses are that it refers to the medallist Leone Leoni.

In Moretta da Brescia's portrait (1530–40) a young man is posed in his finery with head on hand in traditional melancholy pose. Attached to his hat is a plaque engraved in Greek with the message 'I desire too much', which can also be read as a girl's name, Guiglia. The symbolism seems to be telling us that the young man has been plunged into despair because he is not getting the response he desires from this girl. The very graphic pose would have been well understood at the time.

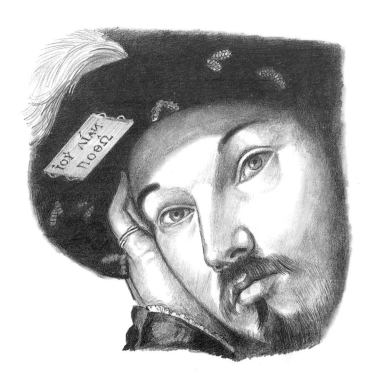

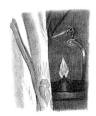

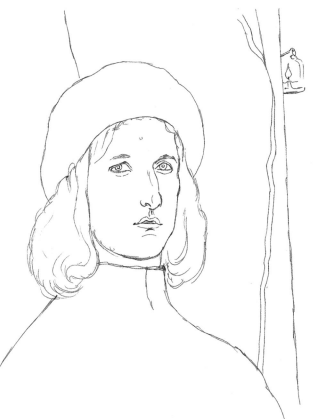

The main point of this picture by Lorenzo Lotto (1506) is to show the symbolism in which even what seems a relatively blank portrait setting can be transformed by the right touch. Behind the rather plain youth is a white curtain which to the right side is slightly disturbed, showing behind it in a dark space a small oil lamp which is burning brightly but not too noticeably. So, 'do not hide your light under a bushel' would seem to be one message. The hidden light behind the pale façade of funeral cloth might allude to the eternal flame of the soul, which continues after death.

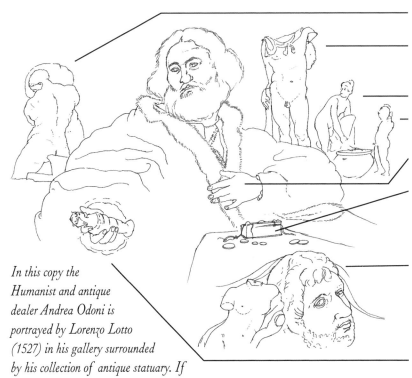

Statue of Antaeus
wrestling with Hercules.

Hercules wearing the skin of
the Nemean lion, though minus
his head.

Venus bathing.

A Hercules 'Mingens'
(Mannikin Pis).

Gesture of 'sincerita', showing
reverence or deference.

Book and coinage or
medallions which were
great collector's items.

The torso of Venus snuggling
up to the head of the Emperor
Hadrian emerging from beneath
the tablecloth is calculated to
have a comic effect.

Egyptian-style statuette of
Diana of Ephesus. Significant
because there was widespread
interest in ancient Egyptian hieroglyphics
as a source of wisdom.

In this copy the
Humanist and antique
dealer Andrea Odoni is
portrayed by Lorenzo Lotto
(1527) in his gallery surrounded
by his collection of antique statuary. If
we look more closely we find that Lotto has chosen his
props cleverly and that they are not calculated solely to
indicate Odoni's prestige. All relate to the humanist
interest in ancient Mediterranean civilizations, some of
them ironically. There is perhaps also a warning against
the collecting of worldly treasure.

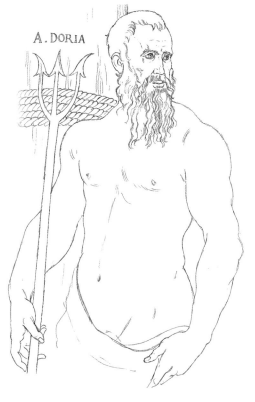

A . DORIA

Andrea Doria was a Genoese admiral and statesman
who defeated the Turks in several maritime battles.
Bronzino portrays him as Neptune, stands him before a
ship's mast on which his name is carved and has him
holding a sail around his loins. As the original (1535)
was an official portrait, it is interesting that the admiral
should have agreed to appear as the Sea God rather than
wearing the usual garb of the powerful. On the other
hand, this approach does rather suggest that Doria exists
in a realm beyond that of ordinary leaders.

Modern Values

In this first example of modern symbolism, the figures are very expressive and expressionistic, as many American works were at this time. The reduction in physical solidity emphasizes elegance and vibrancy.

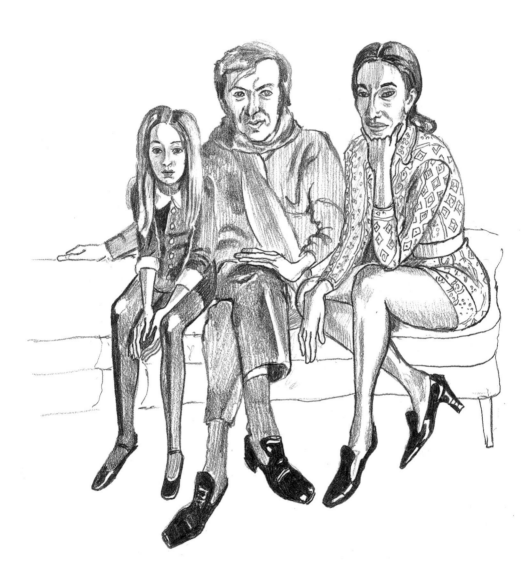

Alice Neel's 'The Family' can be read as a genuine exposition of the values of the New York artistic scene in 1970. The girl and the woman share many traits that set them in their milieu: long hair, long sleeved short-skirted dresses, thin pared-down legs and elongated fingers. These point to a specific view of cutting edge fashion. Although less obviously trendy the man is part of the same scene, with his casual scarf, longish hair and long hands with thin fingers. Posed close together, the three of them eye us unflinchingly and not favourably. Their look says, 'We are here, notice us'. Their slightly angular shapes heighten our awareness of their significance as representatives at the cutting edge, more so than their features or what they are actually wearing. One feels that after seeing this picture the sitters would probably grow to be more like Neel's depiction of them.

The significance of the Goodman picture below would be lost on most viewers. The symbolism relates directly to art itself and the fact that this is a modern version of a school of painting last seen in revolutionary France at the beginning of the 19th century.

Harking back to the work of earlier artists is a constant theme in the history of art. Most artists have taken this path at some point, as a way of discovering new possibilities in their ways of working. The insight gained by trying to incorporate a work that you admire into your own can be of immense benefit to the development of your own style.

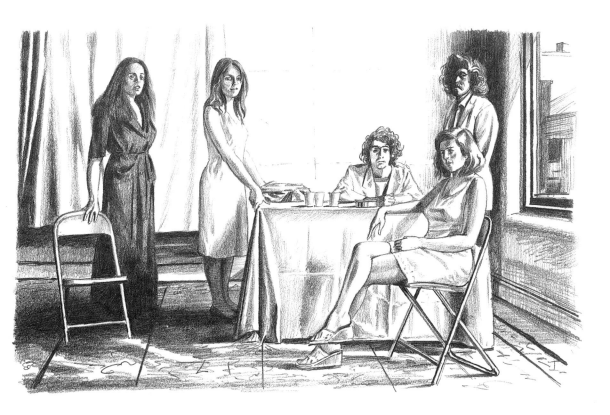

In this copy of Sidney Goodman's 'Portrait of Five Figures' (1973) we see a neo-classicist emphasis on what is a very contemporary composition. The effect with the carefully arranged figures is akin to that achieved by the 19th-century French painter Jacques-Louis David in a painting called 'The Death of Socrates', which is grouped and lit in a similar way. However, in this example the people are looking at the viewer, so it is obviously meant to be a portrait rather than a depiction of an historic event. In another bow to David, this time to his portrait of Mme de Vernice, Goodman has also put in a seated figure.

By using the techniques and qualities of early 19th century French painting in a portrait in which the sitters are shown in contemporary dress supported by contemporary furnishings, Goodman seems to be prompting anyone with enough knowledge of art history to make the connection.

Self-portraits

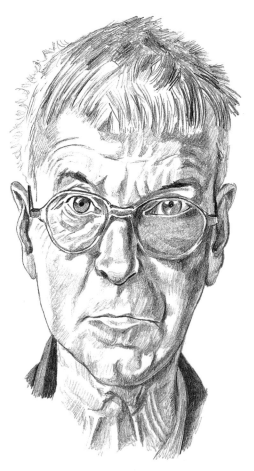

𝒜RTISTS ARE THEIR OWN easiest models, being always around and having no problem about sitting as long as they like. Some artists, such as Rembrandt, have recorded their own faces from youth right up until almost the point of death. Drawing yourself is one of the best ways of learning about single portraits, training your eye and extending your expertise, because you can be totally honest and experiment in ways that would not be open to you with most other people. Quite often with friends or acquaintances you cannot tell the whole truth as you see it, because it might be too devastating a revelation for the sitter. However, with your own portrait you can proceed on a course of investigation to discover all the methods of producing a subtle portrait in some depth. Only you will know what you are seeing, and if the result is none too appealing you don't need to show it to anyone.

One of the most interesting aspects of exploring your own facial features is that each time you do it, you meet a new individual, still you, but different. As you progress you will take more from each new attempt to draw yourself, and find more subtle ways of depicting expressions as well as the ravages of time. You will be amazed by the depth of psychological insight that can be gained from continual study of a person you thought you knew.

Try portraying yourself in as many different mediums as possible and see how far you can take the likeness both physically and psychologically. What you learn by drawing your own face in various states and at various ages will expand your skills when drawing others.

Posing for Yourself

The most difficult aspect of self-portraiture is being able to look at yourself in a mirror and still be able to draw and look at your drawing frequently. What usually happens is that your head gradually moves out of position, unless you have some way of making sure it always comes back to the same position. The easiest way to do this is to make a mark on the mirror, just a dot or tiny cross with felt-tip pen, with which you can align your head. You might ensure the mark falls between the centre of your eyes, corner of an eye or your mouth, whichever is easiest.

You can only show yourself in one mirror in a few positions because of the need to keep looking at your reflection. Inevitably, the position of the head is limited to full-face or three-quarters left or three-quarters right of full face. In these positions you can still see yourself in the mirror without too much strain. Some artists have tried looking down at their mirrored face and others have tried looking upwards at it but these approaches are fairly rare.

If you want to see yourself more objectively you will have to use two mirrors, one reflecting the image from the other. This way you can get a complete profile view of yourself, although it does make repositioning the head after it has wandered out of position slightly more awkward. However, this method is worth trying at some point because it enables us to see ourselves the right way round instead of left to right as in a single mirror. It will also give you a new view of yourself.

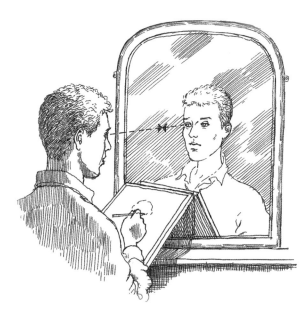

Drawing your own reflection in a mirror is not too difficult, but you have to learn to keep your head in the same position. It is very easy to move slightly out of position without noticing it and then finding your features don't match up. Use a marker spot on the mirror and line up something on your face with it.

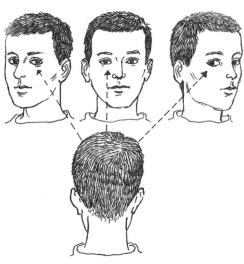

The angles of looking are restricted and whichever way you turn the eyes will look straight at you. This means there will be a similar effect in your finished drawing whatever the angle.

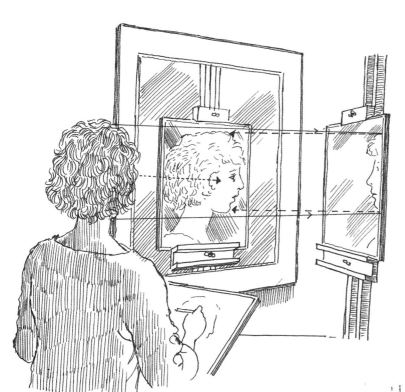

Using two mirrors in order to draw your own profile image. Rarely do we see ourselves in this perspective, so it can be quite interesting visually.

Although a self-portrait is often just an exercise for the artist to learn how to draw, it can also be useful in pictures of large groups. Many Renaissance artists painted themselves into their large-scale figure compositions, partly because they wanted to include a signature but more importantly because a face shown looking out at the viewer – as in this detail from a Botticelli – helped to draw the viewer into the picture.

Individual Viewpoints

On the next two spreads you will find a selection of artists' views of themselves. Included is a mix of artists but all have taken a particular attitude and in some cases give very unusual images of their personality.

They play with different methods both in the actual handling of the portrait and in their attitude to its meaning. Some are very honest and straightforward, others more symbolic and mysterious.

The man in a red turban (1433) has been fairly convincingly identified as Jan Van Eyck, whose work it is. If this is the case, the painting is one of the earliest known self-portraits. The way the eyes sum up the viewer is very much the stare of someone producing a self-portrait. Van Eyck was renowned for his meticulous approach and we can see this in the care that has gone into getting the shape and form of the head and head-dress precisely.

Dürer started producing self-portraits in his youth. In this example he has taken up the pose of a Christ figure, which was probably one he used as a basis for his religious images. The long curled hair, the hand over the chest and the direct look that takes in all it sees without being judgemental combine to make a picture of power and elegance.

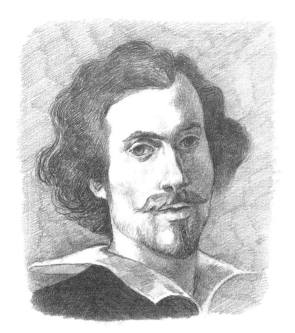

Gian Lorenzo Bernini (1624) shows himself in sombre mood. The rather shadowy soft look to the picture suggests that he is taking a romantic view of himself, but it is beautifully observed and the use of light and shade masterful.

In this rapid and lyrical drawing the artist, John Vanderbank (1750), is almost looking back at us over his shoulder. Although it may seem a difficult pose it is quite common in self-portraiture where, if the artist is using a drawing board on an easel, he has to look across his shoulder in order to see his reflection in the mirror.

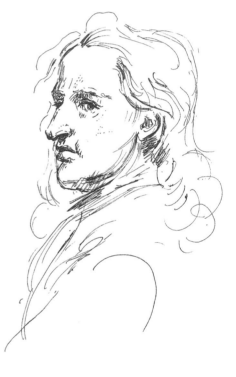

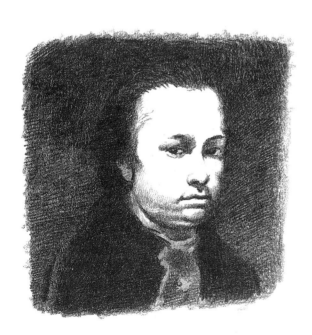

The original of this penetrating self-portrait by Goya (1771) was produced fairly early in his career and is a good example of his 'no holds barred' approach. Here he was not afraid to reveal every defect of his own physiognomy – the slightly pudgy, pale complexion and slightly disgruntled expression – and point them up by providing a contrasting dark background.

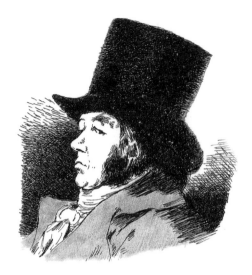

Goya again, in this example looking sideways at himself (1799). The original etching on which this copy is based was produced much later in the artist's life and gives a very clear idea of his rather quizzical and wary personality, although not of the deafness which was besetting him with difficulties. The inclusion of the hat is interesting because its sheer size must have caused problems when he was drawing himself.

Peter Blake was well schooled in traditional techniques before he made his name as a Pop artist. His self-portrait with badges (1961) could be read as an ironic comment on formal approaches to portraiture.

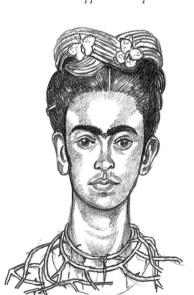

The artist Frida Kahlo was married to Diego Rivera, the most famous Mexican painter of the 20th century. She drew herself in every conceivable situation and never painted anything without including her own image at the centre. Each one of her portraits conveyed some deep psychological view she had of her own sufferings in symbolic form. In this example (1940) she shows herself wearing a thorn necklace.

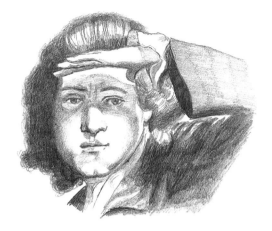

The First President of the Royal Academy, Sir Joshua Reynolds (1747), is shown here peering from under a raised hand, shielding his eyes from the light. This is not an easy pose for the self-portraitist to draw, but it probably appealed to Reynolds as an opportunity to show how expert an artist he was. It certainly makes an unusual portrait.

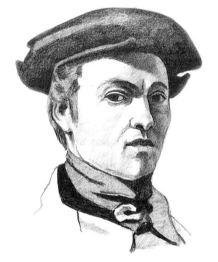

The young Camille Corot (1835) here portrays himself in a dark hat as though poised for painting. His vigorous and economical style gives a very clear and direct view.

Gwen John produced the original of this while she was a student at the Academie Carmen in Paris (1899). She comes across as very self-possessed and confident, even challenging. At the time of this portrait she remarked that 'shyness and timidity distort the very meaning of my words in people's ears. That is the one reason why I think I am such a waif.' So does this self-portrait represent bravado or the real woman?

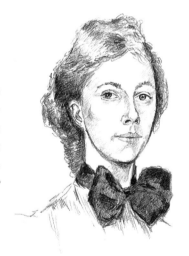

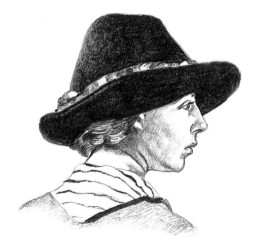

Two aspects in one of British artist Dame Laura Knight (1913). The bohemian rakish hat and loose sweater seem at odds with the well drawn rather elegant profile and look of penetrating attention.

185

The contrast in this series of self-portraits is between emotional power and imagery and total objectivity. The copies of Gauguin and Van Gogh are marvellous examples of the portrait as self-investigation, whereas the Wadsworth, Fry and Roberts epitomize the detached quality that comes out of a portrait where the artist is not concerned with personality. Their concern is more with exploring technique.

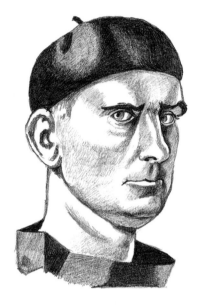

The rather wary expression in this self-portrait by Edward Wadsworth (1930) is partly due to the artist having had to look out of the corner of his eyes to see his reflection in the mirror while he drew at an angle to his vision. This is a good example of the often awkward poses artists have to adopt in order to portray themselves. Wadsworth has concentrated on volume rather than subtleties of outline, hence the rather solid look to the technique.

Roger Fry was the most famous artist to emerge from the Bloomsbury Group which dominated British artistic life in the early part of the 20th century. In this portrait (1926) he appears to look right through us, making a rather strange impression.

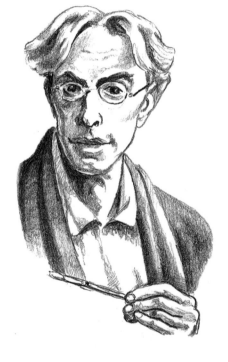

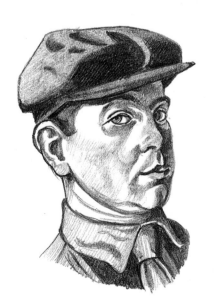

William Roberts' method of drawing was similar in some ways to Edward Wadsworth's but with even more emphasis placed on volume. Here the artist identifies himself with the working man, a persona he projected frequently (1931).

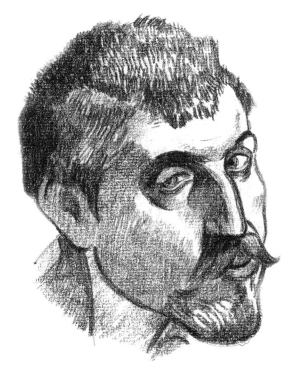

Gauguin gave the original of this chalk copy (1888) to Van Gogh as a gift. He called it 'les miserables', a reference not only to the traditional poverty of artists but also to their bondage to the quest for perfection.

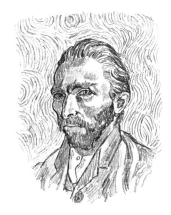

These two self-portraits by Van Gogh (1889–90) give us some insight into the artist's frame of mind in the last year of his life. In the first (left) he is shown bleakly regarding himself, without a trace of compassion, in the recovery period after his terrible act of self-mutilation. The second copy (above) is of the last self-portrait he ever painted, in shock from the death of his beloved brother, Theo, and holding on desperately to his sanity. The resolute face staring out of the the swirling background seems to predict the last despairing weeks of a man driven to the edge of existence.

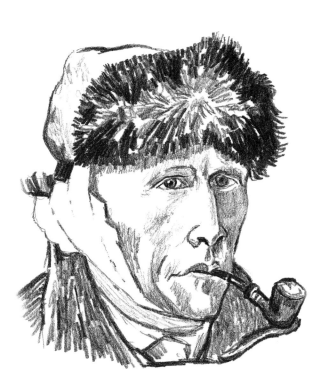

Taken together these portraits relay some basic truths about the art of the portraitist. In the two Spencers we are confronted by penetrating honesty; in the Melendez by a plea for a chance to work more fully; and in the Hockney we appreciate how maximum effect can be achieved through minimal means.

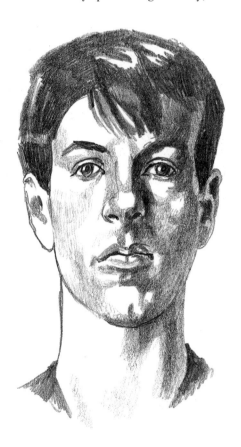

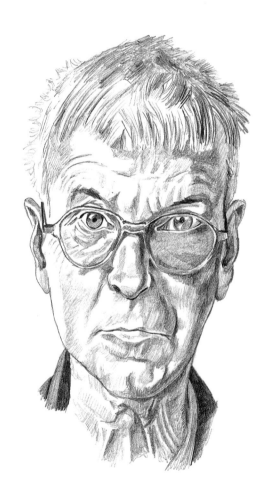

These portraits represent two different stages of Stanley Spencer's career, but despite the distance of 46 years between them both demonstrate the artist's honesty and his lively interest in the visual world he was recording. The younger Spencer is portrayed as a more expectant and confident individual. The second drawing was done in the year of his death and there is a clear sense of mortality as well as humility.

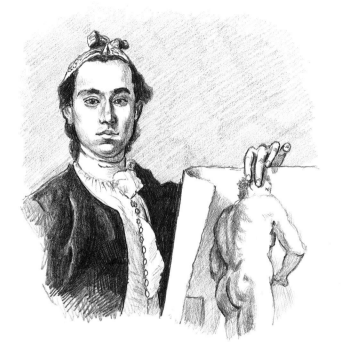

Luis Melendez was a brilliant still-life painter in 18th-century Spain who never succeeded in reaching the heights of artistic achievement. This self-portrait (1708) looks like an attempt to convince his public that his drawing of figures is a good reason to let him move into the more lucrative and prestigious area of history painting where the human figure was the main feature. Notwithstanding the skill evident in this portrait, he was denied the chance by the Spanish Academy and went on painting mainly still-life subjects.

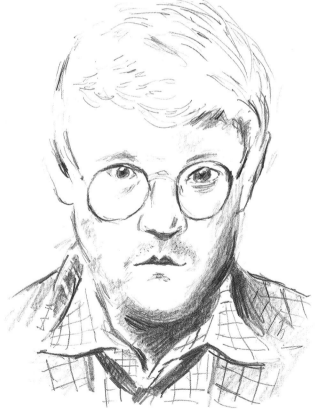

One of the most successful of contemporary artists, David Hockney has been able to follow his delight in drawing the human face in an age when many artists have all but forgotten how to even produce a likeness. In this copy of an original he made in 1983, the intense gaze makes it clear that he misses nothing. His handling of the form is very spare and yet highly effective.

The great challenge to every portrait artist is how to achieve a well-drawn image that is never dull. This next series of examples demonstrates how even a slight oddity can bring freshness to a portrayal.

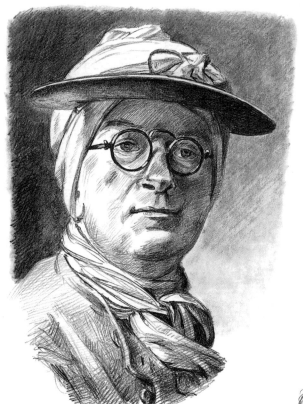

Before the 20th century very few people in portraits were shown wearing glasses. It is very difficult to believe that the painting from which this drawing was made was actually produced in 1771, by Jean Simeon Chardin, so modern is its feel. Chardin painted at least three portraits of himself wearing glasses. Here we see the artist working, spectacles perched on his nose and an eyeshade casting a shadow across his upper face.

One of the most famous of 20th century British figurative artists, John Ward has chosen to portray himself in profile for this self-portrait (1983). He has found a brilliant way of conveying vivid animation and a business-like approach through the pose (the balance of the poised brush and palette, the half-glasses perched on the nose, like Chardin) and the dress (formal jacket and tie).

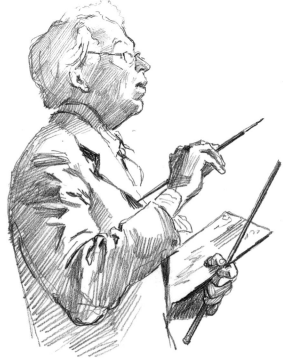

In 'Self-Portrait in Grey Pants' (1992) William Beckman has produced an uncompromising but strangely theatrical effect purely by virtue of the pose.

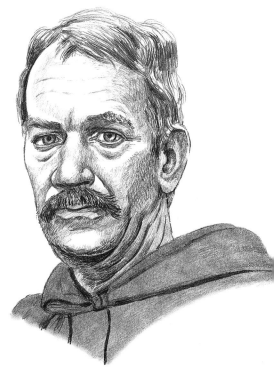

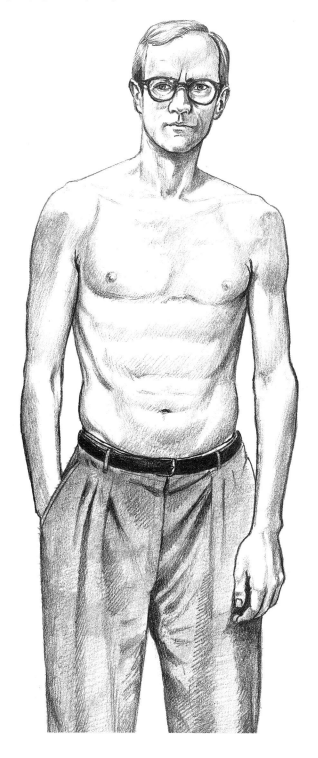

There is a strong, honest realism in this portrayal by American artist Gregory Gillespie (1993). The creased neck and slightly downwards look suggest that the mirror must have been placed slightly lower than his head. The fleece jacket with hood gives a rather austere monkish look to the portrait.

Novel Approaches

When an artist draws himself using a mirror, quite often he sets up the pose to enable him to make a detailed study of the face he is so familiar with. The serious practising artist will experiment with this set up so that he comes to see himself in a new way. In the following series of examples we suggest approaches that will give unusual views and the potential for producing interesting results.

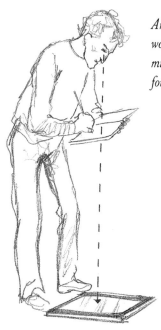

An obvious recourse would be to place the mirror in an odd position, for example on the floor.

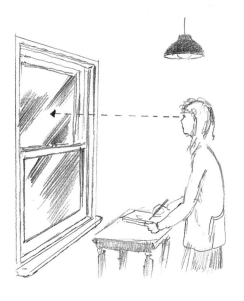

You know how sometimes you catch a glimpse of yourself in a shop window? Well, you can produce a similar image of yourself by, after dark in a well-lit room, drawing your reflection in a window. With this approach you can see objects through the glass at the same time as reflections in it, and this can make for very interesting compositions.

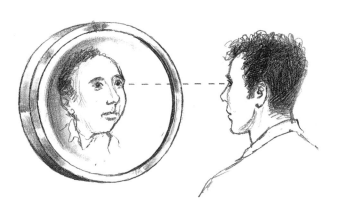

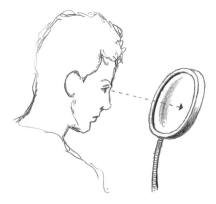

Artists have often had recourse to drawing their reflections in a convex mirror, which distorts what is seen in an interesting way.

A shaving mirror might also provide intriguing distortions.

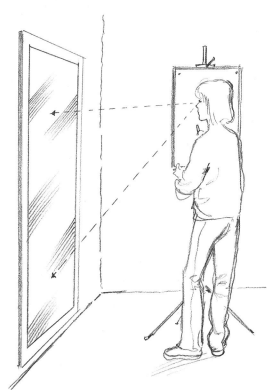

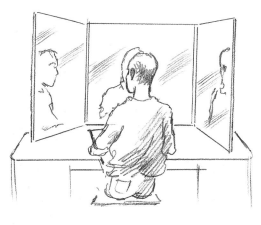

The typical dressing-table mirror could be a good way to get three different views of yourself at the same time. It is also invaluable for a profile view.

A full-length mirror will give another view of yourself and is useful because of this.

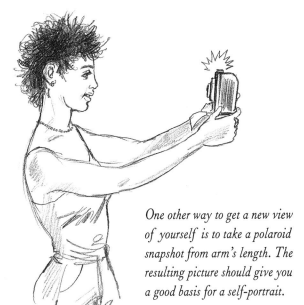

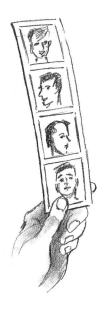

One other way to get a new view of yourself is to take a polaroid snapshot from arm's length. The resulting picture should give you a good basis for a self-portrait.

A variation on the polaroid approach is the multiple passport type photograph that you can take of yourself in a photo-booth. The results are often quite unexpected. Be sure to adopt slightly different angles for each of the shots you are allowed.

Caricature

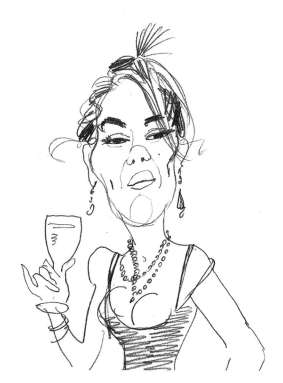

*T*HE ESSENCE OF CARICATURE is exaggeration. You have to take whatever you are drawing beyond the bounds of reality to an area of extravagant shapes. A nose, a mouth, an eye become enlarged marks to express particular types of features. Nearly always one feature is picked on to set the shape of the face and is therefore more strongly marked than the rest, but sometimes a more general effect is called for. For example, the most obvious characteristic of a person might be their 'busy-ness', and so an all-over effect of movement in the figure would be more characteristic than just pointing up one feature.

A caricaturist's dream face usually has a good big nose, or a jutting jaw, or an extraordinary hairstyle. These can be exaggerated so that they are at least twice as big as their normal proportions. Always draw the feature you have decided to concentrate on first, and then fit the others around it. If this doesn't work, it is because one of the other features needs more exaggeration or you haven't drawn the shapes correctly. It is vital to observe the particular shape of the feature in order to bring that person to mind.

Caricature is a fairly cruel medium at its most powerful, and so if you are drawing your friends you should be careful exactly how far you take your exaggeration. Otherwise be prepared to lose friends. That said, it is much easier to draw a caricature of someone you know well because the insights you have can give more edge to your portrayal.

What you must avoid is a formulaic response, which can be quite good fun but is hardly perceptive. When you first attempt this way of drawing you will have to keep changing your image until you get something that people recognize. One of the best tests of a really good caricature is that everyone recognizes the person except for the victim himself. This is one type of drawing where your vision needs to be as much like everybody else's as possible.

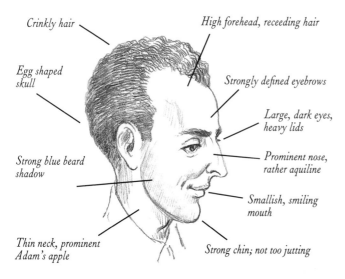

Crinkly hair

Egg shaped skull

Strong blue beard shadow

Thin neck, prominent Adam's apple

High forehead, receeding hair

Strongly defined eyebrows

Large, dark eyes, heavy lids

Prominent nose, rather aquiline

Smallish, smiling mouth

Strong chin; not too jutting

The Process of Caricature

Every attempt at caricature begins with detailed study of the subject's facial features and an assessment of the relationships between them. Your observations will provide clues as to which parts you should exaggerate and which you should play down.

In this first exercise we are going to take a subject and put the features together in such a way that we end up with a reasonable result. Look at the sample face (left) – what do you see?

When you have assessed his features, look at my stage drawings below.

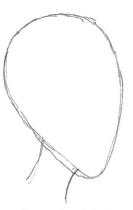

An egg-shaped skull attaching to a rather thin neck. Draw this shape first.

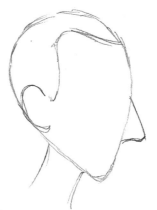

Look at the way the hairline recedes from the forehead. Work this in.

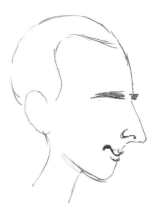

Draw in the eyebrows strongly in thick black lines Put in the prominent nose, making it larger than i is in reality. Give it a smooth, aquiline curve.

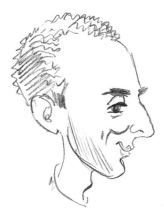

Place the ears well back. Don't make them too small. Add a dimple to increase the smile. Put tone on the jaw to suggest beard shadow.

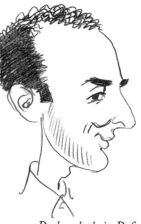

Darken the hair. Define the chin.

Bringing out Characteristics

Caricature provides a very good test of whether you have a talent for observation, which is vital if you are to produce effective drawings of this type. Effective draughtsmanship is important but having a vision of the essential components of a face and how they reveal character is the only way to become an accomplished caricaturist.

Now let us look at a few more very simple examples, this time putting in the basic shapes of the heads. Notice their characteristics.

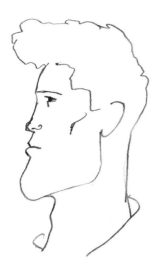

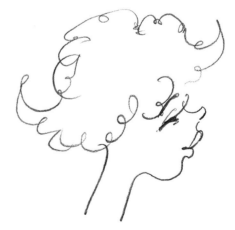

This young man looks rather strong and chunky with curly hair.

Make the curly hair much more obvious by giving him an abundance of it towards the front of the head. Don't draw too many lines, just an outline. Keep the nose small, slightly reduce the depth of the forehead and make the jaw longer, squarer and more prominent. In a way, the hair and the chin mirror each other and in comparison with them the other features appear small and neat. Make the eyes smaller, and show them half-closed as though squinting against the sun.

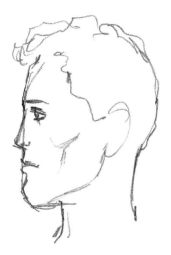

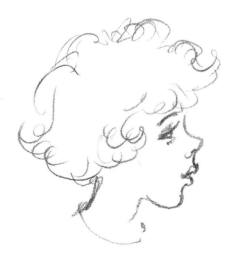

The look here is gamine and perky.

Give her a mop of curls. Don't use too many lines, more a very curly outline as before. Keep the face small but turn the nose up extravagantly. The eyes can stay

large and lashy. Keep them smiling, fairly closed and with a crease beneath the lower lid. Make the upper lip larger than the lower, sticking out a bit. Keep the chin soft and round, and the neck really thin, like a stalk.

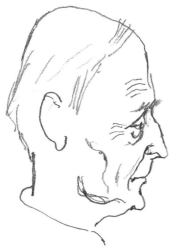

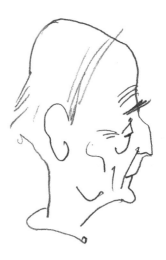

The shape of the bald head is important here and gives the basis of the drawing.

Draw the head with a few sparse hairs, then the ears, large and long. Make the eyebrows stick out. Draw the eyes very small; give them droopy lids and bags and wrinkles to the side. Make the nose even more hooked than it is in the straight drawing, but don't take it too far. A large nose has the effect of strengthening the face, and as this man looks rather frail such a feature would be inap-

propriate. Show the mouth sunken back behind the line of nose and chin. The line of the mouth should be straight and down-turned. The chin should be small but stick out, to make it appear as though he has lost most of his teeth. Next, put in long vertical lines denoting the cheekbones and creases around the mouth and nose. The thickness of the neck should diminish from where it joins the head, to make him look scrawny. A soft droopy edge at the angle of the jaw will complete this picture of old age.

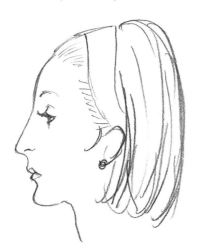

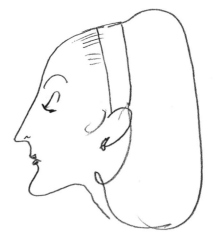

The slightly disdainful or snooty look of this sophisticated woman has been accomplished by making the eyes heavily lidded, the eyebrow arched and thin, the nose aquiline and the mouth small and pursed.

Draw the hair shape very smoothly, in one or two simple strokes. The plainness of the hair-band adds to the

sharp, smooth look. Now put in the high domed forehead but without exaggerating it. The nose must be increased in size in the face and in prominence; keep it looking sharp. Make the eyes all upper lid and give the eyebrow one smooth thin curve. Reduce the size of the mouth and push out the chin without making it too sharp.

Formulas for Features

As you go around observing people you will notice that there are only three or four different types of features. Once you become familiar with their characteristics you will be able to place them in one of these categories for use in a caricature. Of all the features the hair offers the most permutations. Below we show three fairly obvious versions from which many variations could be developed.

Noses

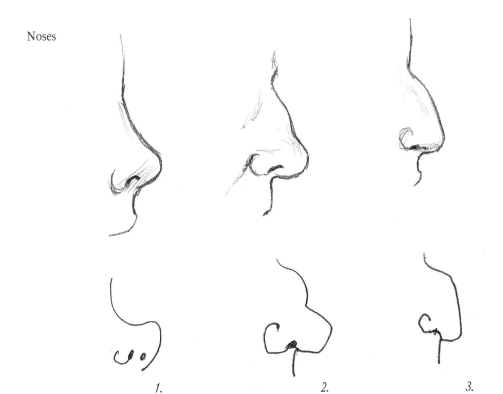

1.   2.   3.

1. Retroussé or turned-up. Draw this version repeatedly until you can do it with ease. Then practise drawing it larger, smaller, rounder or sharper.

2. Knobbly, possibly broken. This type is in some ways easier to caricature than the turned-up nose. Don't be afraid to exaggerate the bumps.

3. Hooked and eagle-like. Don't be subtle at the outset. Try for a pronounced downward point. You can modify your drawing, making it rounder or sharper, depending on your subject.

Eyes and Eyebrows

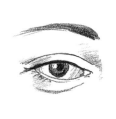 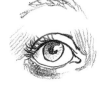 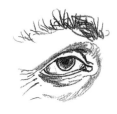

  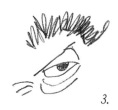

1.   2.   3.

1. Almond shape, almost oriental. Keep the lines very thin, simple and dark with the iris and pupil shown as just a black disc. Draw the eyebrow strongly but make them thin and long.

2. Round and open, probably light coloured. This type needs to look very open, with the iris not touching the edges of the eyelids. Show a few eyelashes sticking up and reduce the fair eyebrow to almost nothing.

3. Tired eyes, showing signs of age. The shape of the eyelids is important: capture the droop towards the outer corner, ensure the lid half obscures the dark disc of the iris, make the lower lid droop significantly and add lines for bags and side wrinkles. Use scribbly lines for the straggly, bushy eyebrow.

Mouths

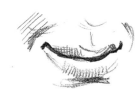 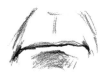

 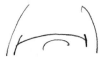

1.   2.   3.

1. Smiling, youthful mouth. A grin line will do for this, with two corner creases to emphasize good humour.

2. A grim mouth is almost a reverse of the shape for the smiling mouth, but straighter. Use sharp, thin lines with two etched creases either side.

3. The full outline of female lips can be kept quite simple, but make the top lip equal in thickness along its length and the bottom lip rounder.

Hair

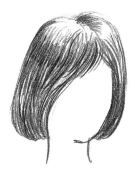

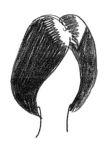

A smooth cap of dark hair brushed down and curling under. This is drawn almost as a black single shape with just a dent at the top for a parting and curving round the head. You can leave a small gap of light at the top to show a shine, but this is not imperative. The outline should be quite smooth.

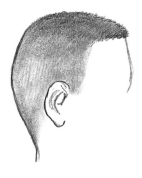

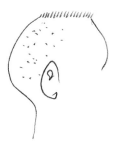

A shaven head with just a short cap of stubble on the top. Draw this as a line of short stubble-like grass on the top of the head, then add just the shape of the skull with a few dots to show the hair is shaved.

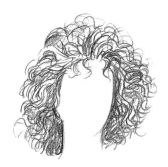

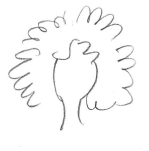

A wild curly mane of a hairstyle. This can be simply shown by making a quick scribble of springy-looking lines. Make sure there is enough space to suggest a lot of hair around the head.

Photo Opportunities

Photographs are a good source of opportunities for honing your skills as a caricaturist.

The original photographs from which the following series of drawings was made were all prize winners in a competition run by the National Portrait Gallery of London. Such was the high quality of the images that I was able to deduce a great deal about the individuals and distil this information in a few lines.

For this next exercise, study my caricatures together with the drawings I made from the photographs, and then cover up my attempts and have a go at doing your own versions.

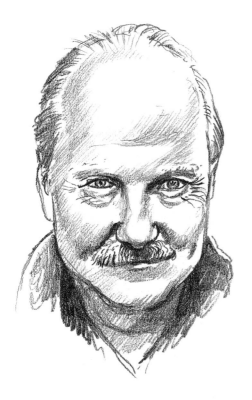

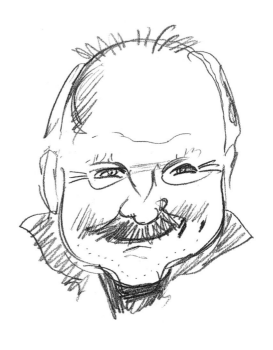

The drawing emphasizes the sparseness of the hair on the top of the balding head and gives plenty of expanse to the forehead. The eyes are squeezed horizontally with sideways laughter lines clearly shown. The knobbly nose with the bristling moustache is a great asset for the caricaturist. Rounded cheeks with laughter dimples and a suggestion of stubble on the chin complete the picture.

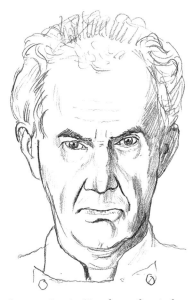

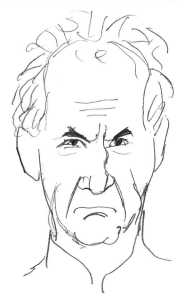

This rather truculent looking face, of a chef, was lit very harshly to bring out the grooves of the face. Like the first example, this character had a sparse crop hair at the top of a receding hairline. The forehead corrugations, the dark, diabolic eyebrows and the narrowed eyes are all

shown sharply and simply. The large knobbly nose is not as obvious from the front as it would be in profile. Make the most of the deep hollows running the length of the cheeks and the grim downturned mouth with creases from nose to mouth.

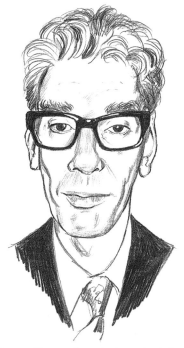

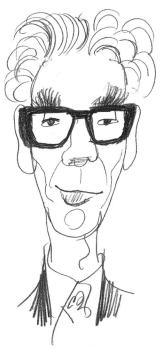

The long face and heavy-rimmed glasses lend themselves to extension and emphasis. The rather tousled hair is a good feature to emphasize as are the bushy eyebrows. The heavy lidded eyes, the blunt nose and the lop-sided mouth

are all put in with minimal lines. The mouth was tilted a bit more than it appeared in the photograph. The lines around the mouth and cheeks are telling, as is the prominent Adam's apple.

Photo Opportunities

When you've tried the previous exercises it would be worth seeing how far you can produce a caricature in one short sitting. You'll need to co-opt family, friends or colleagues to sit for you. Start by taking photographs; then, if the drawings don't quite work, you will be able to rework them with the help of your photographs later. Bit by bit you will start to get the images to work. Don't be afraid of exaggeration, and keep your drawings simple.

With these next images we are going to take the imaginative process a bit further by looking at full-length caricatures.

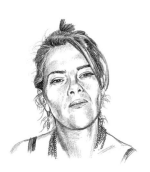

The face of artist Tracey Emin is a gift to any caricaturist, with the slightly scruffy hairstyle, narrow eyes and dark eyebrows, turned-up nose, and the largish chin. The upper lip appears slightly fatter than the lower one and so is ripe for exaggeration. The cheekbones and dimples can be accentuated. The almost falling-off dress showing her figure goes with the long legs and a rather awkward tottering stance to play up her tendency to fool around. The glass of wine in the hand helps to complete the image of a keen party girl. I couldn't remember whether she smokes so I left out a cigarette. If she does it would help build the picture even more, rather as it did in the image of Sylvia von Harden on page 162. Tracey Emin is a brilliant symbol for the 'Brit-Art Crowd'.

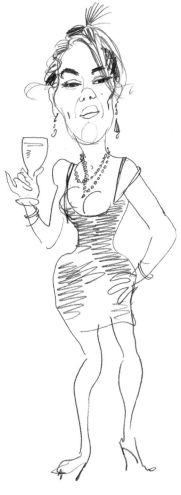

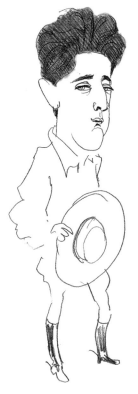

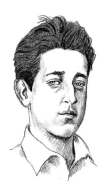

I had only this Spanish rider's horse, hat and shirt to give me clues as to an appropriate stance for him. He looked rather aristocratic, rich, and haughty and so I worked on this idea, giving him smart white jodhpurs, shiny boots and a self-regarding pose. Features-wise I emphasized his luxuriant hair, the length of the rather fleshy face with soft cheeks and rounded chin, and enlarged the aquiline nose. The upward-slanting eyebrows aloft heavy lidded eyes complete the picture of natural hauteur.

Caricature as Art

Now a few drawings from one of the first really brilliant caricaturists, Henri Toulouse-Lautrec, who made it into an art form. He revolutionized the art of lithography and even when painting full-blown oil paintings tended to edge towards the caricature side of portraiture. The originals of these examples of his work were intended as caricatures and are powerful linear statements of character.

These two self-portraits (right) are brilliant parodies. The portrayal of himself with spurs and whip addressing a large friendly cow was used on an invitation to a party. The other was a scribble of himself on a spare sheet of paper.

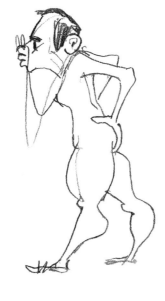
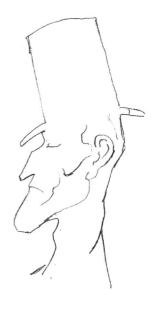

These graphic caricatures of performers Valentin-le-Desosse and Yvette Guilbert were produced for posters advertising various shows and showplaces. Yvette Guilbert complained about her image, but it was instantly and universally recognized. And, for a caricaturist, that has to be the highest compliment.

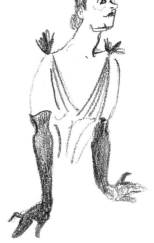

Pushing your Limits

Chuck Close, an American painter, produces portraits of an immense size. They are often in style similar to the passport photograph that you would get from a photo-booth, but drawn about five or six feet high and with meticulous attention to photographic realism. Their combination of heroic-sized proportions and meticulous miniaturist technique produces monumentally powerful images.

You might find the idea of trying this for yourself rather daunting. In reality, I think you will find it very liberating and immensely rewarding.

The simplest approach is first to project a slide photograph of your model, to the largest size you feel you can handle, onto a wall covered with cartridge paper. Draw your model in outline so that all the proportions are correct. When you have done this, forget the slide and turn your attention to the model. With them in front of you, proceed to draw the portrait up, using the outlines to ensure you get the shapes right. See how far you can take the detail, especially the hair, which can be very difficult at this size. The most fun comes when you start to draw the eyes and mouth and have to transfer what you see to such an immense size.

Good luck and enjoy yourself. You'll probably surprise yourself with your skill.

Chuck Close 'Leslie', 1973
Original: watercolour on paper
184 x 144.6cm (72½ x 57in)
Pilloburg Family Collection,
Fort Worth, Texas

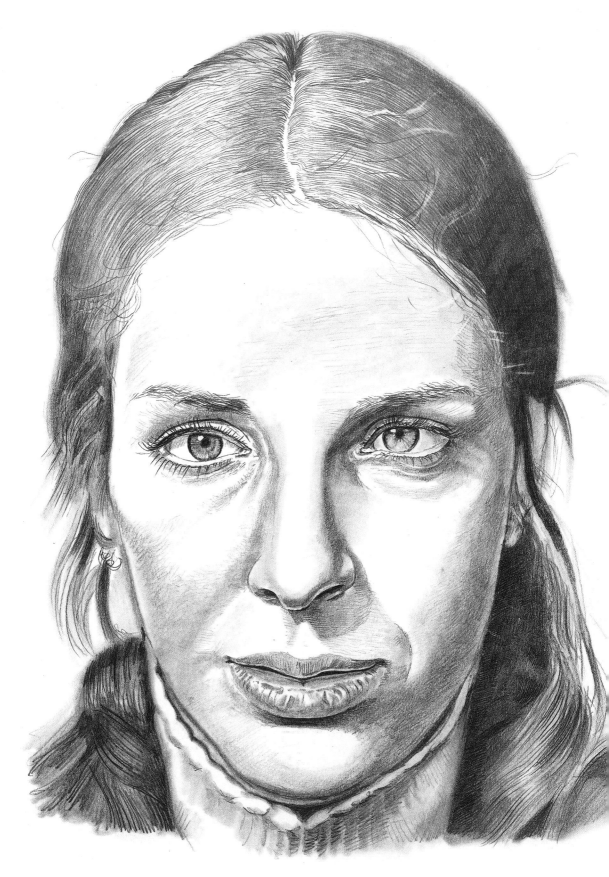